MW00679623

Napoleón Gómez Urrutia

Before the
Next Revolution

Politics, Progress and the Future of Mexico

Napoleón Gómez Urrutia

Before the
Next Revolution

Politics, Progress and the Future of Mexico

Before the Next Revolution
© Napoleón Gómez Urrutia and International Labour Media Group
All rights reserved

First edition: April 2017
ISBN: 978-0-692-86481-4
Cover and interior design: Angelica Bistrain
Typeset in accordance with the law.

No part of this publication may be reproduced without the written permission
of the author.

Printed and bound in the United States of America.

*To my family, for their tireless support and remarkable courage
throughout this long and complex struggle.
To my other family, Los Mineros of Mexico, for their tremendous
bravery and loyalty. To our brothers and sisters of the United Steelworkers,
who have supported us unconditionally from the beginning.
To workers around the world, who have stood in solidarity.
To all who risk their lives each day in the hope of raising up our nation.*

And to those who believe that a better future is possible.

Contents

Introduction
One Hundred Years after the Revolution

This book is a collection of many of my articles that have been published in *La Jornada* in Mexico as well as various interviews in other media outlets, from 2011 to 2017. The great majority of them have been edited or updated. Some speak to the timely context in which I wrote them, but almost all remain current given the political and socio-economic climate. Published together, they reflect my analysis and perspective as an economist, social activist and trade union leader, and present an approach to understanding the recent changes that Mexico and the world are experiencing, as a result of the unjust and senseless exploitation of natural resources and the labour force at every level.

This edition presents an analysis of our present reality and draws a number of vitally important conclusions, in addition to identifying and calling out those responsible for attacks against the working classes and in particular, Los Mineros, one of Mexico's most democratic and independent trade unions. Naturally, the themes of globalisation, international trade agreements and treaties, and conservative and capitalist politics and tactics are dissected for their negative economic effects on various segments of society. Millions of our citizens are unjust victims of a pernicious wealth concentration that benefits the few; we as a nation remain impoverished, suffering from ever-increasing income inequality and a slew of political challenges both inside and outside our borders, all of which we must confront.

Overall, the writings published in this work were intended to denounce the abuse, corruption and impunity that so sadly and shamefully prosper in Mexico. The crux of the content was not only to draw attention to the responsible or guilty parties, but also to propose changes and measures that would have an impact on the country and society's direction and destiny, to contribute to resolving the problems faced by Mexico and other countries that find themselves in similar circumstances, by seeking to build a new model of development and shared prosperity.

During the last five years, over which these articles, columns, interviews and opinion pieces were published and distributed, the impacts of the global financial crisis have remained constant across a whole range of economic sectors. I have often tried to unpack the similarities between Mexico's problems and those faced by other Latin American and European nations. In Mexico's case in particular, Vicente Fox and Felipe Calderón's PAN party (Partido Acción Nacional) governments have come to an end (2000-2012), and seemingly so have their influence.

The prevailing model, however, has continued to operate under various guises since the PRI party (Partido Revolucionario Institucional) regained power in 2012, offering hope that the catastrophic period of the PAN governments, with their climate of incompetence, insecurity and irregularities had been overcome with the change of administration and the arrival of Enrique Peña Nieto. Naively, it was believed that the PRI party's return to government in 2012, a party we had endured for 71 years, broken only for the 12 years of the PAN party rule, would somehow change the country's direction and destiny.

Nor have we seen any resolution of the conflicts and aggression against the working classes who make up Mexico's free, democratic and independent trade unions such as the miners, electricians, teachers, rural workers, indigenous people, students, young people, women who have suffered domestic violence and other public sector groups and organisations, such that there is now real frustration, resentment and profound mistrust among the majority of the public towards the government, towards arrogant, callous businessmen as well as towards the most conservative sections of the church and the nation's religious fanaticism.

Running in parallel to these conflicts, Mexico's economic crisis has sharpened and there is no clear prospect for when its inhabitants will recover their purchasing power and wellbeing, which would make it possible to imagine a change of direction and strategy, towards a more equal society. In this period of decline and failure, which has been accompanied by the introduction of a policy privatising the country's energy resources, the issue of inequality is inextricable from Mexico's economic activity and political life.

The increasing concentration of wealth is a key issue and cannot, nor must not, be ignored. Nobody can deny that there is now a great gulf that radically divides those that have the most, known as the 1% of the population, from those who have least, the 99%. These different sections of society have radically different lifestyles, concerns and problems. Equally, their aspirations and expectations are completely contradictory, along with their aims and goals. **Inequality is a subject that divides, not unifies.**

When deciding on the selection of the chapters and articles that would comprise this book, it was clear that those studies concerning exploitation of the workforce and natural resources could go unheeded if they are not properly evaluated and their harmful effects for society are not quantified, in terms of both the means and the methods companies use to maximise their profits and benefits. These effects include the terrible, often irreversible, expense of dispensing with ecological concerns, damaging the environment and negatively affecting the health and lives of workers.

Across the world today, and particularly in Mexico, politicians and corporations urgently need to make the system more efficient and set out defined parameters for a new, improved and more fair economic rationale, as well as establishing laws and norms that clearly define the legal framework of their behaviour, at the same time as they set out their conduct and social responsibility, changing and correcting the very structures that underlie production and wealth creation.

Although all economic agents, companies and governments do interact and communicate directly with one another in society, this often involves ties of complicity and corruption, and in practice on a day-to-day basis laws are not obeyed and the rule of law is frequently flouted. This is true both of parties from government and business interests failing to demonstrate genuine respect for their political commitment and social conscience. This leads to many directors of companies and authorities, generally the most dishonest, who act with impunity.

In 2013, my book *Collapse of Dignity* was published, which, based on the reactions it received, had an impact on many Mexicans and international leaders thanks to its serious and responsible analysis of the facts and tragic events denounced within its pages, but also due to the accusations it made and documented, which have sadly still not been set right. The improper relationships maintained by the government or the people who direct and control the dominant economic and political system not only generate a climate of continuous impunity, but also allow very little room for society to renew and transform itself towards a new model of growth where justice, respect and dignity prevail.

Collapse of Dignity is not simply a book about denouncing corruption and political persecution. It is also a cry of indignation and a call for change, an appeal to the social conscience of Mexico and the wider world. The text and its thesis are fundamentally a voice of hope, for society to change and avoid the attacks of ambitious, immoral, cowardly and malevolent people. This book was read by hundreds of thousands of people from different backgrounds and countries, which turned it into a national bestseller, widely sold and distributed according to *New York Times* figures. It was also published in various languages: English, Spanish and French, with Russian, German and Chinese editions currently under revision. That the book struck such a nerve is a validation of a shared, global concern about human dignity and social justice.

In Mexico we continue to see abuse and crime committed daily, with people being able to do little to prevent or alter it or at the very least to call it out with any possibility of success. This is why people continue to feel frustrated by the indifference and callousness of many politicians and members of the business class. The voices expressing criticism and desperation are growing daily, because this situation seems endless. In fact it seems to be getting worse, pushing people to the very limits of exasperation.

This is apparent in the inadequate justice system that seems to have no control over, nor any response to, the lack of transparency and bias. **As I have articulated, a country that does not respect the rule of law is a country headed for the failure** of its government and institutions. Thus conflicts are drawn out and everyone takes advantage to get better benefits, meaning the struggle for human and labour rights goes on and the only people who do not seem to realise the severity of the situation are those in government and their cronies from the world of big business, who only act in their own self-interests.

This means that not only do they renege on the promises they made, but they also cast public office and professional ethics into disrepute, whilst causing hurt and offence to the victims of this system of unrestrained greed

16

that disregards the great majority of the population, often behaving as if they were their enemies.

Currently, Mexico is suffering from serious issues related to security, unemployment, marginalisation, poverty and the lowest salaries across Latin America. The growing inequality that this model has created urgently requires a change of strategy and policy, towards one of greater shared responsibility and prosperity. Even the distribution of revenue has deteriorated to such an extent that the country now has one of the highest levels of wealth concentrated in the hands of ever fewer people or groups.

The Mexican government persists in an economic and labour policy that is causing worrying rises in inequality, exploitation and sustained deprivation under a system of employer protection contracts, on top of which many companies and organisations operate fake unions, rendering this a way of life. Currently, Mexican workers' salaries are 40% below their Chinese counterparts, when comparatively 10 years ago they were almost three times greater.

One of the negative aspects of Federal Labour Law that still exists is the obligation for unions to be registered and authorised to operate by the Ministry of Work, meaning unions require ministerial approval before they can legally function and before leaders and unions alike can fulfill their responsibilities to their members. This mechanism is obviously obsolete, because it is a hangover from the fascist regimes of the last century, in Germany, Italy and Spain, which allows the government to maintain political control over trade unions and to recognise only those which are sympathetic to them, or which do not represent an obstacle to their interests. This mandatory requirement to comply with the *'toma de nota'*[1] utterly contradicts the spirit of Convention 87 of the International Labour Organisation related to the freedom of association.

We must not forget that **in Mexico the practice of criminalising labour demands and trade union action is commonplace,** by labour dispute matters being arbitrarily turned into criminal cases. This is a dis-

....

1   'Taking note' (official recognition of the union's registration)

tortion of the correct application of justice, a perversion of the legal framework and a violation of the Political Constitution of Mexico.

But there is still time to set things right and change our course. We urgently need to implement democracy, respect the rule of law, revolutionise society and find the best strategy and the true political will to transform the our nation's destiny, with honour and dignity.

I am sure that the articles compiled in this book, which are mainly the fruit of five years of journalistic collaborations and interviews, will support the efforts called for by our times: to find a better way, and to preserve our great social wealth as working people and as a free and democratic nation.

One hundred years have passed since the violent Mexican Revolution. Today, we owe it to ourselves and to the memory of our ancestors to fulfill their promises for true change. Ours is a moral and intellectual revolution, and we will achieve the transformation of society only when we realise our ability to build a future together, using alternative solutions that work for the betterment of all.

I. The Failure of Government

Government Failure

The almost 12 years that have passed under the incompetent governments of Vicente Fox and Felipe Calderón, from 2000 to 2012, can be summed up in a single word: failure.

Both governments have failed the country and its people. The economy has shrunk rather than grown, and has been provided with no real opportunities for progress. In political terms, our unstable democracy has become the sum of the interests of an elite, which can hardly be said to cover the full range of social forces that exist in Mexico. In terms of social affairs, poverty and the unfair distribution of wealth have become drastically worse, coupled with the application of laws that have hit working classes, widened the jobs gap and left large sectors of the population to seek refuge in the hostile and uncertain informal economy. In terms of employment, where Calderón has continued to irresponsibly apply the anti-trade union politics of his predecessor Fox to attack independent and democratic unions, both presidents having employed contemptible characters like Francisco Javier Salazar and Javier Lozano Alarcón to do this. In terms of education, which has seen nothing but attempts to privatise public education at elementary, middle and higher levels, opening up the possibility that future generations will not be protected by education and will be forced to enter the dangerous world of violence and delinquency. In terms of international relations, where previously the prestige of Mexico commanded respect but today has been replaced by the degraded image of a government that doesn't know what its objectives are, much less its goals, and which lacks a vision to steer the country towards sovereignty, justice and wellbeing.

Unfortunately, there has been a huge and perverse complicity in this process of decomposition in the last 12 years. The loss of value of the Mexican economy over the last decade, which went from 9th to 14th in the world, compared to Brazil, which went from 15th to 6th in the same period – just as Carlos Fernández Vega has signalled – clearly shows the collapse of this government and of the National Action Party.

Macroeconomic indices and widely circulated international studies on Mexico's national performance leave no room for doubt about this terrible frustration and decline. This is because these two governments have acted in favour of a single sector of society, namely businesspeople, and inside this sector, a small group whose members have monopolised economic power and have illegally taken control of the country and the weak minds of politicians. A government that only acts in favour of one sector and never listens to the majority voices in society in order to move in the correct direction or straighten out crooked paths cannot call itself a government, much less a successful one. It has instead acted as a simple administrator or manager of private interests that have manipulated and used it as a puppet.

The more than 120,000 deaths in the war on organised crime during the last presidential term indicate the failure of this campaign, and more precisely the failure of a police regime as opposed to a democratic one, with the aggravating circumstance that the basic human rights of Mexicans are not respected. Many outspoken voices have pointed out that this huge military and police operation has the unwritten but clearly identifiable aim of intimidating and restraining popular protests against high living costs, social injustice and widespread corruption.

And there is no way to escape this reality. The government's latest gesture in its shameful subjugation to large private interests is **the swift approval, between December 2011 and January 2012, of the Public-Private Associations Law, with which the government not only irresponsibly prevents the State acting as a State**, but also hands over to big businesses the vital task of building infrastructure for national development, with conditions that are more than abusive for public resources. **The same has happened with the indiscriminate handing over of the country's non-renewable natural resources such as minerals, oil and gas to Mexican and foreign private companies.**

There is no national problem that does not reveal the government's wholesale failure. The fact cannot be ignored that responsible, authoritative voices have signalled this collapse day in day out, and the people who have fallen victim to it have protested. This means that the entire nation must respond by adopting new policies that imply a radical change from the government's neoliberal economic model which both Fox and Calderón, and before them Salinas and Zedillo, have imposed on the country.

Social and economic forces must immediately abandon their indifference in the face of this misplaced government strategy and begin to develop a politics that fully reflects our true national interests, to the exclusion of no one. This will be the only way for Mexico to return to the path it never should have left, that of efficiency, fairness, shared social responsibility and nationalist politics, which with all its defects was an efficient and authentic guide for Mexico's progress.

Mexico's Destiny

What is at stake in the current electoral campaign is the possibility of a return to being a viable nation with purpose, with a future. This campaign will define Mexico's destiny. Elections are being held for the Presidency of the Republic, the Senate and the Chamber of Representatives, as well as governorships and local councils. The whole country is shaken by this political reality, which will last until June 1, and will then unfold according to the electoral results. It is true that the so-called political class is obliged to address national rather than personal interests, but they must also recognise the interests of citizens and different social forces.

Everyone senses that a real change is needed, not a regressive change as Mexico suffered from 2000 to 2006 under the disastrous leadership of the National Action Party, but moving forward instead, under other party colours that can be none other than those opposing the current conservative government and which have a chance of winning.

Unfortunately, during this electoral contest overviews and generalisations of projects have been presented, but it is obvious that most of them are not supported by a clear plan with objectives and strategies that will enable those goals to be achieved. The media, with only a few exceptions, merely reproduce isolated phrases, images and messages that do not deal with the root of the problems that the country faces in striking out in a new direction as a viable and truly democratic nation. They often give the impression that they bank on disorder, on confusion and on deception so that things stay as they are and thus they can reap greater benefits.

People have understood during these weeks of electoral campaigning that if things go on as they are, the regime of privileges for the most economically powerful and disrespect for the legitimate interests of large swathes of the working class population will continue. Or indeed we will continue to experience the bloodshed that has gone on since 2006, under Felipe Calderón. The same with limitless unemployment, the high cost of living, or the inflation which constantly eats away at the miserable annual wage increases, which are promoted by the government to benefit the wealthiest in society, or even the neglect of the needs of the largest sectors of Mexican society, including the neglect of education, culture and science, and the lack of meaningful campaigns to fight poverty and hunger, work which cannot be substituted with welfare programmes or opportunistic economic stimulus plans.

The most serious problem of all is that Mexico needs a radical change in its social and economic model to one in which new production and work relationships are based on very clear concepts of social responsibility shared between all sectors of the country. This would require the nation to move towards a new Social Pact which balances inequalities, or as José María Morelos has said, which moderates indigence and opulence. This is the path of salvation for Mexico. There is no other.

Mexico needs to change its traditional neoliberal strategy, which is based on the intensive exploitation of the working class and natural resources as well as the concentration of wealth in the hands of monopolies. It needs to adopt a new philosophy of labour that posits business owners and workers as equals, based on respect for workers' interests, so that both groups participate more actively in productive decision making and in strategies for action, always according to a balanced way of thinking that truly values productive commitments. In other words, we must write a new National Plan, because at the moment there is no agreement to command and guide efforts to guarantee economic growth and social development, rather the country is steered by the interests of a small group of business owners and bankers, who are arrogantly called "free market forces".

It is absolutely necessary to build a new politics which constitutes the base and the core of economic growth, job creation, productivity and wellbeing of the huge majority of the population. Other countries such as China, India, Brazil, South Korea, and before them, Japan, have brought about changes in their economic and social structures, worker participation in productive processes has grown, with higher wages and a resulting increase in demand, and a fairer distribution of wealth. Mexico abandoned this drive and now has the lowest economic growth rate in Latin America, lower even than countries like Haiti, which is surviving despite disastrous circumstances.

The results are patently clear. In Mexico the system of brutal exploitation of the workforce has become more acute, while in those countries, as in many others, the rules of the game have changed and they have progressed. True democracy cannot and must not remain anchored in political-electoral processes, instead it must advance towards total social reform. For business owners and for workers, a fairer model of shared social responsibility has great benefits.

The main thing that needs to change is Mexico's obsolete and inhuman economic system that concentrates wealth. This issue must feature in what is left of the electoral campaigns of the various presidential candidates, if this political competition is to be a true, constructive reflection of real points of view held by the Mexican electorate, in which the desire to serve, and a passion for and dedication to the struggle for dignity and justice predominate.

Calderón and the Trans-Pacific Partnership

Next Monday, April 2nd, president Barack Obama of the United States, president Felipe Calderón of Mexico, and the prime minister of Canada, Stephen Harper, will participate in a North American summit in Washington, DC. It is expected that at this meeting they will analyse issues such as the role the three nations will play at the summit in Cartagena, Colombia, which takes place at the end of April, Mexico's conduct as host and member of the G20, which will meet in June in Los Cabos, Baja California Sur, and the Mexican government's application to join the Trans-Pacific Partnership Agreement (TPP), which is not yet finalised.

Negotiations concerning this Trans-Pacific Partnership Agreement are underway at a critical time for the global economy, which in many areas has faced catastrophe due to the lack of control, recklessness and irresponsibility of financial markets. Global unemployment is currently calculated at between 250 and 300 million people and in Mexico almost 6 million people are unemployed, a figure that does not include the 14 million in unstable informal employment. Most governments and international financial institutions are pressuring for debts to be shouldered by workers, and of course anti-union currents are going so far as attempting to wipe out the unions, especially the most democratic ones, so that no organisations are left to protect and defend workers' and human rights, and thus passing the responsibility for and consequences of the crisis and their abuses onto the working class. This is a myopic, clumsy and incredibly short-term vision.

International federations such as the American Federation of Labor and Congress of Industrial Organizations (AFL-CIO), International Metalworkers' Federation (IMF), and the International Federation of Chemical, Energy, Mine and General Workers' Unions (ICEM), among others, have signalled in writing and across a range of forums that the Mexican government should not be allowed to join the TPP until it changes its economic and social policies to ones that truly promote economic growth, employment, the correct application of justice and respect for the unions' autonomy and freedom.

The members and leaders of these strategic and powerful federations are conscious of the importance of global commerce. They also know that **free trade agreements have not improved the wellbeing of the world's workers, nor have they contributed to decreasing inequality between and inside different countries.** Commerce should be fair and based on the principle of equity if it is to increase living standards, quality employment, social protection and security, at the same time as defending workers' rights, avoiding contamination, and respecting human rights, dignity and democracy.

Felipe Calderón's administration has been seriously questioned by these and other organisations, but this questioning has become more forceful in the face of the administration's recent application to join the TPP, the lack of coherence in the objectives it announces and the specific negative results that can be observed in terms of the application of justice, inequality, corruption, and repression of workers and democratic unions.

In the eyes of the global federations, it is clear that the Mexican government, as a member of the North American Free Trade Agreement (NAFTA), has not respected the parallel labour cooperation agreement, has failed in the protection of workers' basic rights and has been highly inefficient and insensitive in relation to their concerns about excessively low salaries, employment insecurity and the growth of employer protection contracts and ghost unions, some of which are linked to organised crime and others of which have ties with or are part of 'official or charro' corporatist unions. These are generally fraudsters working with government consent and at the service of employers to ensure that wages and working conditions are minimal, in a truly scandalous and shamefully barefaced system of corruption and complicity. For all these reasons the global organisations oppose the Mexican government joining the TPP.

Even worse, Calderón's labour policy has led to greater repression and violence through the use of physical intimidation and terrorism against the activists and leaders of democratic and independent union organisations. His government has abused its power by employing methods such as official recognition or 'taking note' against democratic union leadership, with a discriminatory strategy of controlling unions that do not serve their interests. In the desperation of his anti-union policy at the end of his six-year Presidential term of office, with clear fascist overtones, Felipe Calderón has gone as far as pressuring and forcing representatives and senators to approve his labour reform project, which deepens exploitation, inequality and insecurity in Mexico.

The esteemed columnist and labour lawyer Arturo Alcalde Justiniani is entirely right in asking: when will the government will stop siding with the corrupt leaders it protects as if they were a necessary evil? **When will it end the war against the mining union and stop putting all the power of the State behind Grupo Minero México?** This is the reality of governmental policy towards Mexican workers. In short, **Calderón would rather look after investors than his own citizens.**

Labour Reform and Criminal Negligence

In recent weeks PAN (National Action Party) and PRI (Industrial Revolutionary Party) leaders have repeatedly mentioned, ignorantly and in bad faith, that this September members of both parties in Congress will approve a labour reform that no one knows the details of and which therefore seems suspicious. This does not herald anything good for the working class. They guarantee that these are campaign promises which we all know the candidates made to themselves and their accomplices, with serious lack of responsibility towards the Mexican people.

Some of the aforementioned people have signalled that we need a labour reform, because they say that to the contrary we will be hindering the country's progress and the growth of the economy. As a result, they argue, insufficient jobs will be created and there will be fewer prospects for development, which according to them will only be achieved with this projected labour reform.

The noteworthy aspect of this issue is that representatives and lawyers for the Coordinating Business Council (CCE) are meeting with leaders from the Confederation of Mexican Workers (CTM) with the aim of reaching agreements on this labour reform project. They are not publicising the content of their analysis or deliberations, which gives rise to doubts about the true nature of their meetings. The CCE and CTM dare not expose such information to public scrutiny as they should rightly do in relation to such an important issue for Mexico's economic, political and social development.

What seems obvious is that these two groups mean to reach agreements in the name of the whole country and all social forces, and this goes no further than being a sham to reach mutually beneficial deals. This is because the CTM no longer represents anyone in the realm of workers' organisations, only the inner circle of its formal leaders, fossilised in the image of a power that they haven't had for decades. Businesspeople, then, are negotiating with a group that only represents itself, not Mexico's millions of workers, and much less those who are affiliated to the country's autonomous, independent and democratic unions. Among those excluded are miners who have faced unrestrictedly depraved political persecution, students, *campesinos* and holders of shares in common lands, telephone operators, tram conductors, electricians who were hit by the arbitrary and unconstitutional disappearance of Central Light and Power, teachers and many more besides.

It seems obvious that that union representation, which long ago was an authentic campaigning force, is now disarmed in advance by its lack of worker authenticity and of solid democratic leadership. Its countrywide policy is one of submission to business owners, as well as governments, with no regard for their partisan or ideological ties. In each work centre where workers make a serious attempt to gain authentic representation for the legitimate interests, CTM representatives appear to place themselves at the orders of bosses and oppose the legitimate interest of true workers to influence them, threaten them, beat them and criminalise their efforts.

In this supposed labour reform project, which is in fact a labour contra-reform, promoted by CTM representatives, the suggestions made are: to give total flexibility to bosses to hire or fire employees without any responsibility falling on the company; to accept or reject union representations; to legalise outsourcing and protection or ghost unions; to heap a huge number of complicated requirements on exercising the right to strike so that in effect they wipe it out; to affect unpaid salaries such that the constitutional right to strike, universally accepted as a prerogative of workers to oppose the injustices of companies, becomes only a legal declaration with no real effect.

With these arguments, it is unquestionable that the CTM is meeting with members of the CCE simply to identify the anti-union policies of the outgoing PAN governments, which today they want to lumber the next government with. In this they ignore the fact that in other countries around the world where counter-reforms have been applied, such policies have now been reversed, since in fact it became evident that those sell-out projects were not viable. Examples of this are Spain, where unemployment reached 25 percent, or Italy and Greece which are now in the midst of deep social crises. While there they are returning from the neoliberal venture of suppressing authentic union rights, in Mexico there is an insistence on this path of social suicide.

This phenomenon has repercussions in other areas of working class life. If the country's labour laws are not adhered to, many workers who fulfill high-risk roles are left completely unprotected, such as in mining, where for example in the state of Coahuila alone 150 people have died in six years due to the criminal negligence of employers and the federal and state governments that cover up for them. If all the mandates of the Constitution's labour laws were carried out, none of these tragedies would have happened. In coal mines, companies as well as authorities prevent unionisation and worker protection. In the face of these tragedies, no one does anything to correct or prevent them, as shown by the explosion in February 2006 in mine 8 at Pasta de Conchos where 65 miners died, with those responsible remaining unpunished. **If we carry on this way there will be more industrial homicides. For this reason we urgently need to draw up and promulgate laws that penalise the criminal negligence of companies and gives exemplary punishments to those responsible, be they investors or government.**

Attempts to bring in labour counter-reform, on one side, and corporate impunity, on the other, are two sides of the same coin: that of corruption on the part of government and antisocial companies, which Mexico should not be willing to tolerate any longer.

Betrayal and Crime against the Working Class

More and more individuals and organisations are clearly speaking up against Felipe Calderón Hinajosa's labour reform project, and those voices are getting louder every day in their protests at the indifference and stubbornness of the government and many representatives and senators. Disagreement and indignation are rife in Mexican society. This odious initiative clearly demonstrates the political irresponsibility and the deep hatred that the current president has for the Mexican working class. We can easily make out his submissive partiality to business interests, which in Mexico have grown thanks to exploitation of the workforce and natural resources, so that a few people accumulate the wealth that should be fairly and correctly distributed across the nation.

A commission of the 61st session in the Honourable Chamber of Representatives has rushed to have a report on Calderón's proposal ready, and this will be viewed in the light of the **discontent that the initiative has sparked, due to its obvious intentions to condemn workers to veiled slavery**, the effects of which will explode like a social time bomb for the next government. It would be as enormously irresponsible an act as Felipe Calderón's if the new government, which comes into office on the 1st December, were to assume this rightly renamed contra-reform as its own. Some of its supporters have no idea or pretend not to know about the sinister results this will have for social peace in Mexico, and they obstinately pursue their despicable efforts to have it approved.

This is happening because they have refused to study the failure and negative results that similar measures are currently bringing to countries like Greece, Spain, Ireland and Italy, or brought to Latin America in recent years. **These countries are trying to claw their way back from where we in Mexico are being led.**

This new attempt at aggression against workers and unions is the product of the class struggle, but in this case it is reversed: not to favour wellbeing, but to move back in time to the elitist regime of Porfirio Díaz, when the huge majority of Mexicans were held down by the ruthless exploitation on the part of rich and insensitive landowners. We are facing the bleak perspective of a return to 1910. Historically, what Calderón, his political allies and their bosses, and businesspeople are trying to do is a disgrace.

This is a seriously bad prospect for the Republic, as is the fact that Calderón's odious initiative does not propose an employers' and government reform, which are so urgently needed, to change the ideology of unchecked personal ambition against the solidarity between Mexicans, and bring to legal order the business sector, institutions and politicians who profit from exploiting the workforce and for decades have abused their privileged position.

Employer and government reform are absolutely necessary for the nation's health. The outrages frequently committed by many businesspeople and innumerable public servants in their role as employers, not only against workers but also against the nation, have for years been a cause for great concern. The drain of capital out of Mexico is one of these outrages, with resources that stemmed from abusive exploitation of the workforce and the overlapping of governments in this damaging practice, which means that capital goes to finance the growth of other economies and leaves ours abandoned to its fate. The very low taxes that powerful companies pay is a further abuse, whereby even governments award them benefits, giving them back huge amounts of the very low rate of tax that they pay to the treasury, with which they favour corruption and trick workers to avoid paying the 10 percent of real profits that the law obliges them to pay. There are examples everywhere. Therefore, we urgently need an employers' and government reform before a labour reform, one that forces businesses to make their real profits transparent and workers' pay proportional to this. The new government must govern for all, and there is no other way to do this than by following this path of action and behaviour.

It is infuriating that many people who are speaking or writing today in support of this initiative are demanding transparency and accountability from unions and leaving employers free from any similar obligation. In those media there is no call for them to be clearly accountable in the same way, comfortable as they are in their complicity with powerful politicians. As for the National Miners Union, known as Los Mineros, from the union's foundation in 1934, we have always been completely accountable to our people, according to our Statutes, because they are the sole depositories of this power, the workers, not an authority that at the very least has always been suspicious in not being accountable to the Mexican people. This is the case of permanent cash counts, the accounting and finance forums carried out by the General Surveillance and Justice Board, as well as the reports that Statutes deem necessary, which demonstrate transparency at every national convention, for the scrutiny and approval of all delegates.

Calderón's initiative is utterly discriminatory. **The fair thing would be if employers were forced to use the same regime of transparency in their management of resources as they are calling on unions to conform to.** The necessary employers' reform must include the obligation for taking note for the leaders of business associations and the business owners they represent, with the aim of finding out whether they all comply with law, if they are transparent and up to date with their tax responsibilities, if they keep their legally binding promises in terms of industrial security and health protection, as well as the ever-absent environmental protection. If they fail to comply there should be genuinely severe prison sentences for the employers or public servants who break the law in any area of national economic activity.

It is a social demand for businessmen to make a commitment to the country, along with the public servants who overlap with them. This is the core of a democratic system, anything else is deception and demagogy which will surely generate serious instability and social crisis for the country. If it should unfortunately occur, **we must never forget the names of those people who, due to personal or group interests, are betraying and acting against the rights of the working class, the population and Mexico as a whole.**

Respect for the Working Class

Mexico's experience over the decades shows us that mutual respect and the fulfilment of obligations must always prevail if a cordial relationship is to exist between business owners and workers. In theory, when one of the parties breaks this bond and stops duly considering the legitimate interests of the other, conflict arises. In practice, it's not workers who trespass the boundaries of law and of constructive coexistence between both production factors. They aren't the ones behind the disputes.

After 12 years of pro-business National Action Party (PAN) governments, the fact of the matter shows that it is employers who most often exceed the limits that should naturally frame relations between employers and employees, making it difficult for the right conditions for developing productive joint labour to be maintained or reached. This was more noticeable than ever over the two PAN six year terms, initiated under the presidency of Vicente Fox, when he defined his as a government "of businessmen, by businessmen and for businessmen", thereby destabilising the balance between workers and employers, a relationship which had already seen sharp indicators of significant discrepancy since the two previous PRI governments.

The government assault on the trade unions was one of the main tactics pursued by the PAN party in power; another was the repeated dismantling of government labour policy to repress the integrity and dignity of workers, a fact attested to by the situations of miners, electricians, aviation employees, *campesinos,* by the absence of a social policy and by the general persecution of any popular demands, whether proposed strictly in relation to employment, or to the declining economic situation of the wider Mexican population.

This is a past that must not be repeated and should not have happened at all. **National progress is based, among other things, on fair, respectful and equitable relations between production factors, and Mexico is a nation not of businessmen, but workers.** The current government seems to understand this and has, albeit slowly, been showing signs that it intends to pursue a policy in keeping with the older – but more valid than ever before – principles of social justice, opposed to which is the complex network of interests and collusion, incubated over at least the past three decades, between private economic power and government.

Currently, there are attempts to change this behaviour, such as the official decision to bring justice to retired electricians regarding the rights that they never lost over their own retirement funds and the *toma de nota*[1] of their legitimate leaders. Another example is the new attitude towards mining workers, expressed by President Enrique Peña Nieto himself, and backed up by the current director of the Ministry of Work and Social Security, Alfonso Navarrete Prida, in a joint press conference with the most important international and national trade union leaders, recognising the legitimacy of our leadership and a decision not to proceed with the persecutory policy against the mining worker's trade. Added to this is the declaration made in recent days by the Secretary of Labour and Social Security's delegate in Zacatecas, Gilberto Zapata Fraire, who used statements to the media to call for mining company bosses in the region to show mandatory respect for workers' rights, and indicated that on this point culture and advice must improve to ensure they adhere to the provisions of Mexican law.

The civil servant conceded that there are serious interests at play for many mining company owners, which abuse workers' rights. These company heads, he said, want to get the most out of an economic activity, to make high profits or bonuses, and in so doing often ride roughshod over the interests of workers.

....

1   Literally 'taking note', a recognition document required under Mexican labour law which recognises trade unions and their leaders.

On this point he mentioned a tug-of-war going on in Peñasquito, which is also apparent in Camino Rojo, Tayahua and other places, where they are seeking to gain an advantage beyond what is legally permissible.

The mining workers' demonstrations of their discontent are, he added, linked to the law which provides for workers to receive a 10 per cent share of profits being broken, as well as violations of collective agreements and the freedom of association, and allegations of threats, heavy handedness and abuse by employers, alongside an even more sensitive issue of sexual assault against female workers.

The current government still has a long way to go in this and other areas. The important thing is that it has already set off on a path that it must stick to, and quicken its pace. The situation in Mexico cannot go on with disputes unresolved, particularly when those disputes have their origins in arbitrariness, arrogance, corruption and political persecution against democratic trade unions and their leaders.

Just as the first article of the Political Constitution of the United Mexican States asserts, **respect for the rights and interests of workers is not simply an employment matter, but also a human rights issue.**

Labour Rights are Human Rights

During the six-year term of Carlos Salinas de Gortari (1988-1994), alongside the devastating privatisation of public sector utilities including mining, electoral and labour rights, along with migration issues, all happened to be excluded from the North American Free Trade Agreement on the basis that this was the compromise needed with the United States government of president George H.W. Bush to fast track the treaty forward in this country. With this, both the assessment of elections and the unrestricted control of matters concerning the relationship between employers and trade unions remained in the hands of the government.

Both facts were highly negative, given that under the appearance of supposed sovereignty in terms of human rights, some, such as electoral issues, remained exclusively in the hands of government, which had not at the time seen the need to move towards a reform that would make elections independent from the interference of executive powers. This separation was only partially achieved later, but labour relations stayed in the hands of state administration in alliance with the powerful sectors of private enterprise.

However, when Felipe Calderón was President of the Republic (2006-2012), the Inter-American Commission on Human Rights (IACHR), a pan-American international body, put pressure on him to integrate human rights as a substantial component of Mexican law, or risk being exposed on the world's stage as one of the few countries to turn its back on human rights. This pressure was enough to make Felipe Calderón's government decide to incorporate them into Mexican laws, and this was officially published on 10th June 2011 in Articles 1 and 102 of the Political Constitution of the United Mexican States. Incidentally, the government did this almost in silence and did not lavish any special celebration on the event.

This act made work rights subject to these two constitutional articles, particularly the first, duly authenticated by the Nation's Supreme Court of Justice, meaning that from that moment labour issues were no longer left out of the Mexican Constitution. Today therefore, as soon as the Federal Labour Board on Conciliation and Arbitrage Committee fails to resolve or pronounce on the demand for the precedence of human rights in the labour legal matter concerned, a worker or trade union can now formally apply to the National Human Rights Commission (CNDH, by its initials in Spanish) to demand that labour rights, which are indeed human rights, are respected. The case may then be taken to the IACHR, whose resolutions are binding and must be obeyed.

As things stand, various government administrative practices in employment matters, along with the Federal Labour Board on Conciliation and Arbitrage Committees, have turned out to be in contravention of human labour rights, and these disputes could be referred to the CNDH for just resolution or advice. This will serve to strengthen the call for the so-called *toma de nota*[2], a merely administrative practice left over from Mussolini's fascist Italy as a means of political control of the unions, to be removed from Mexican Labour Law. The existence of Federal Labour Board on Conciliation and Arbitrage Committees poses an attack on the rights of workers and trade unions, since authorities of executive power act as judge and jury, which are not impartial in their management of labour disputes and controversies, nor in matters of employer-employee relations, and are usually under the control of the business classes.

The removal of the Federal Labour Board on Conciliation and Arbitrage Committees and the *toma de nota* from the Mexican legal landscape has been a demand fairly made by authentic trade unionism. Instead of these institutions, labour courts independent of executive power and belonging to the judiciary should be instituted, which would open up the

....

2 Literally 'taking note', a recognition document required under Mexican labour law which recognises unions and their leaders.

right space for dispute resolution in the area of employment matters, as they will benefit from the contribution of human rights doctrine.

The *toma de nota* is nothing but an unjust administrative recognition by the government of the existence and actions of trade union organisations, and it must be removed for good. **Workers have the inalienable and universal right to govern their lives according to self-determination and should not have to depend on the grace of the government.** This official recognition ruptures the autonomy of trade unions and jeopardises the freedom of association, which are determinations that the United Nations, through the International Labour Organisation, has set out in its Conventions 87 and 98, on Freedom of Association and the Right to Collective Bargaining between workers and employers, respectively.

When complying with the application of human labour rights, Mexico cannot and must not keep turning its back on the infinite majority of nations worldwide.

Mexico's Image in the World

Nearly three decades ago, Mexico belonged to a group of six countries that formed an emerging group of nations with the serious potential and sufficient human and natural resources to become, in a few years, part of today's strongest leading global economies. Their organisation was dubbed the Group flying the banners of Peace and Development, and was made up of Russia, China, Brazil, India, Egypt and Mexico.

They held various meetings, including one under the presidency of Miguel de la Madrid in Cancún, Quintana Roo. In New Delhi in 1986, in my role as Director General of the Mexican Mint, the *Casa de la Moneda*, and as President of the International Mint Directors Conference, I had the personal duty of presenting the Prime Minister of India, Rajiv Gandhi, with a commemorative medal of the Cancún meeting, which we had designed and made in Mexico, along with a personal letter from Miguel de la Madrid. During the ensuing long, friendly and very interesting conversation with Gandhi, I was joined by the distinguished ambassador of Mexico to India, Graciela de la Lama. She helped me to enlighten the Prime Minister about the greatest international competition in the history of minting – to produce two billion Indian coins – which was held by India and won by Mexico's *Casa de la Moneda*, placed first for quality, cost and delivery time over the remaining 11 participating countries, which included some of the most powerful in the world; Germany, France, England, Canada and others.

On saying goodbye, Gandhi, who also simultaneously held the position of Finance Minister, asked for us to have a photo taken together, which we both kept with real fondness and appreciation. Mexico's economy at the time was stable, a product of the previous PRI party governments' policy, with strong state intervention and regulation of the country's most significant production and service industries. The privatisation process of this period had only recently begun to be considered, and although steps were being taken in that direction, the major sell-offs of national companies and institutions that would go on to alter the country's trajectory had not yet been finalised.

What happened next, affecting and altering Mexico's destiny and image, was that it began to adopt a neoliberal development model based on strategies introduced from outside sources, predominantly the World Bank and the International Monetary Fund. Alongside this, Salinas and Zedillo's governments made major concessions to these strategies, which were damaging to the national interest. This was followed by an increase in the handover of companies and banks under national ownership, through shady and underhand deals that allowed significant scope for corruption.

The PAN governments of Vicente Fox and Felipe Calderón, never prepared to govern in favour of Mexico and the Mexican people, expanded on this model with a very makeshift approach. We are living through the consequences today, and most of the population is suffering dramatically. First of all, from serious inequality, exploitation and injustice. Secondly, the gaps in society are ever more exaggerated, as demonstrated by the fact that 300 families hold half of the national wealth, while nearly 60% of a total population of 118 million people lives in poverty. The lack of public safety and the number of murders and kidnappings continue to rise, at the same time as employment goes down and more people become unemployed day by day. There is an obvious lack of opportunities and to top it all, for the majority of the population any hopes for a better standard of living are fading fast. Lastly, the economy is in recession and only grew 1.2% in 2013, one of the lowest rates in all of Latin America and indeed the whole world.

The result has been that Mexico's standing in the world has slipped, and those responsible languish in impunity. We no longer number among the ranks of this group of "emerging or growth" nations, as some economists and political commentators like to call them, as it is now known as the BRICS group and is made up of five countries: Brazil, Russia, India, China and South Africa. After entering a phase of serious decline and domestic unrest, Egypt was swapped for South Africa, and they simply stopped inviting Mexico to take part, in light of its problems in terms of low growth, inequality, corruption and internal social turmoil.

What can be done under these circumstances? The PRI party's return to power has sped up all the reforms that the PAN party were incapable of carrying out – which is not to say they are all good – such as labour, education and fiscal reforms, and the excellent recent energy reform. The question on everybody's lips, with the spirit and hopes of the Mexican people, is whether this package will see Mexico emerge from our current state of lagging behind, stagnation and inequality, or if we are headed downhill instead.

Will Mexico be able to regain the place it once had, its image and standing newly recognised for democracy and freedom, or will conditions become even worse? This is the challenge faced by the current government, which showed a real interest in making these changes happen within a single year. The people's trust will be, as with anything, contingent on achieving positive results; for the good of everybody in society, let's hope that a shift is soon made towards greater justice, equality and dignity. Only then will Mexico recover its political and diplomatic tradition, respect for its national sovereignty and the position it once held on the world's stage.

The Economic Policy of Inequality

An economic and social policy which does not translate into greater wellbeing for the majority of the population is a conservative and ignorant policy that can only lead to greater inequality and the risk of permanent social, political and employment crises which eventually destabilise a country. In Mexico, income distribution has become increasingly unequal, as employment and wages have steadily decreased while the profits of large companies grow exponentially every day.

That strategy has gone hand in hand with the loss of freedom and democracy, as well as the gradual disappearance of the middle class. The fruits of economic growth have been lost over the past 30 years and instability has grown tremendously for Mexicans. The ignorance and ambition of businesspeople and the most corrupt politicians have exacerbated this situation, added to the fact that corporate consolidation, technological changes and the entry into the market and the global economy of millions of workers in China and other Asian countries has complicated the sphere of productive work in Mexico, competing as they do with lower prices and products of only acceptable quality.

The problems Mexico faces have increased due to the low growth rate of the economy, the loss of opportunities, rising unemployment, the dramatic drop in wages to stagnant levels, the increase in poverty and the growth of insecurity. All this has resulted in a terrible decline in Mexico's image abroad and the discrediting of the government, because now not even their changes and reforms generate confidence or any expectation of a real change in society.

Today the labour market has lost the power and ability to generate decent and fair wages. Over 30 percent of Mexicans of working age are unemployed or earn poverty wages. Poverty affects more than half the population and in some states, such as Oaxaca, Chiapas and Guerrero, this proportion reaches two-thirds, double what it was three decades ago. Real wages have stagnated and even dropped to a level lower than increases in productivity, which up until the 1980s had remained close. The income gap has therefore worsened rapidly to the detriment of employees and the population, making Mexico the country with the lowest average income in Latin America, something that is both immoral and utterly unfair.

At this stage it is necessary to increase wage levels, for both minimum and general wages, maintain productivity growth, but through education and training rather than exploitation, and open up more and better job opportunities for women and young people, thereby moving towards a new strategy of shared responsibility and prosperity. **It is not possible to continue with the callous model of growth, which comes with the price of inequality, because the consequences could lead to a real economic, political and social crisis.**

The system of government in Mexico has not done enough over the past 30 years to build a system of social security, tranquility and stability that allows workers and their families, as well as society, to ensure they make progress in life and maintain a prosperous level of activity which would lead to greater welfare, not lesser as is currently the case. This is the real nature of the problem that many people perceive, with the exception of those who have the ability to decide and take action to change the course and destiny of economic development.

It is probably not an issue of lack of ideas or strategies for improving the quality of life of individuals and the working class. It is more likely the result of insensitivity and the lack of a genuine political commitment to implementing the required changes to activity and the structures of production. In most cases, when reforms are introduced, they are purely cosmetic reforms to maintain the privileges of those who benefit from inequality. Or they are measures that are advertised to give a picture of democracy that does not exist in practice. Sometimes, measures that serve only to meet domestic and international pressure, but are never actually intended to be fulfilled, are also applied.

One such case is that of the recently proposed labour reform, in which it is clear that the State is trying to retain control of the working class through maintaining the decadent and fascist system of official registration of unions with the Ministry for Labour, despite this being outdated and contradictory to freedom of association. Another is that the new Executive Power retains control of the new organization of the Judiciary Power, which will supposedly replace the Federal Board of Conciliation and Arbitration, and will leave local boards under the control of governors and local bullies.

In summation, there is progress, but it is of questionable origin and far from transparent ends. **Because if the aim is indeed to democratise Mexico's labour policy**, this should begin with respecting the right to strike as well as collective bargaining and freedom of association in elections and the recounts demanded by workers, increasing wages and benefits, protecting the life and health of the workforce through frequent inspections and forcing companies to comply with the rules and regulations in force. That is not an idealistic model, it is a project for a strategy which is committed to the future of the Mexican people, which can immediately be put in practice if there is political will.

An Ominous Supreme Court Decision

The decision made by the Supreme Court of Justice of the Nation (SCJN), on Wednesday 30th January 2013, with which it revoked the protection of the rights of 16,599 members of the Mexican Union of Electricians (SME), is a bad omen for current and future generations of Mexicans. It means that in our country, the Court can violate labour and human guarantees when a lawful union opposes political decisions that threaten it, and mean serious repercussions not only for its members, but also for the rule of law that should protect the contractual relationships of all workers.

This, alongside other considerations, makes it clear that rights in Mexico are very unstable, above all because this decision was made by none other than the country's highest legal tribunal which has the obligation of complying with the Political Constitution of the United Mexican States. And the same goes as regards the collective and individual labour rights of workers, which that court applauded when they were raised to the status of human rights, a qualification that has been in force since June 2011. The SCJN is the court which, before any other legal instance, should take the utmost care to comply with human rights, a constitutional precept with the clearest and most advanced universal nature.

This decision sets a bad precedent; it means that in Mexico and as a result of technical arguments that have nothing to do with justice or legality, not even the Supreme Court of Justice is capable of guaranteeing validity and balance in the application of the state of law.

This implies that in our legal system employers, the rich and even the government, which wields influence over the whole of society, are not required to comply with the law. They ride roughshod over legality, and impunity has become an almost insurmountable obstacle in the path of applying the law and justice, which should always be approached in good faith.

In our country, then, due to the capricious decision of a negligent ex-president like Felipe Calderón and his pernicious Minister of Work, Javier Lozano Alarcón, they can get away with fact that 44,000 workers could lose their jobs and this, instead of being punished, is praised by the highest legal tribunal.

The position taken by the SCJN has one serious and dangerous implication that confirms, in the current issue with the electricians, the PAN governments' impunity in their irresponsible acts, just as the previous government led by Vicente Fox set out to deny the respect that was due workers and their autonomous and democratic organisations. These include the electricians themselves as well as Mexico's pilots, teachers, farmers and miners, metalworker and steelworkers, who have for almost 7 years been facing odious, merciless and demented political persecution on the part of public power and some companies that lack all conscience of social solidarity, like Germán Larrea's Grupo México.

This political persecution has been demonstrated since the 19th of February 2006 when there was an industrial homicide in mine 8 at Pasta de Conchos, Coahuila, where instead of investigating and punishing Grupo México, the company responsible for the tragedy in which 65 workers lost their lives, Vicente Fox's government and Grupo México threw themselves into the cruel political persecution of the miners' union and their leaders. They hurled false accusations that have to date been legally rejected by all the judges and tribunals who have dealt with the issue, having accurately qualified it as unconstitutional.

It seems that the current Industrial Revolutionary Party (PRI) leaders perhaps fail to realise that they can no longer follow in the footsteps of National Action Party (PAN) governments, in their enmity and severe aggression against Mexico's authentic unionism. Perhaps they do not realise that the party's image deteriorated during the 12 years it was in power, or that they no longer have the strength and unity that they had two or three decades ago, which must have made them react politically which must force them to correct so many previous mistakes committed by the PAN with whom they alternate and who will follow them. Hence the importance of the case of Pasta de Conchos, where they have not even proposed an objective investigation of what happened in February 2006, so as to correctly apply the law and give the mining profession back their dignity and respect which have been trampled by a businessman who acts more like a colonial landowner that the head of a modern business.

It is good that the entirety of the current government, unlike their predecessors, were present on the 31st of January at the site of the tragedy at the Pemex B-2 Tower to pay their respects and show their solidarity with the workers who were killed and injured and their families. But they still need to solve the issue at Pasta de Conchos: relief must be given and justice must be done for the widows and children who lost family members in that industrial homicide. Dealing with this demand would be a clear indication that they are not going to continue down the same anti-union and anti-worker path as the PAN, who seeded insecurity in this important sector of the economy and industrial development in Mexico.

The worst thing about case of the SME is that the Supreme Court's decision not only worsens the image that the rest of the world has of Mexico, but also shows that they are uninterested in protecting the basic interests of workers or a specific union, and that the tendency is to wound other organisations and social sectors which show their discontent with the political decisions that damage their legitimate rights. **As such, it seems that we need another court to monitor and correct the actions of the Supreme Court of Justice so that it applies the law in good faith and correctly makes justice a reality**, to the letter of the law.

Political Will in the Face of Insecurity

The current social and political landscape in Mexico is extremely concerning and should prompt serious reflection and immediate action on the part of the Mexican government, and society as a whole. There have been multiple instances of social unrest, showing that strategies for neutralising each dispute urgently need to be found, from direct bargaining – as has been seen in the case of the dissenting students of the Instituto Politécnico Nacional – to dialogue, political settlements, and even punishment with the full force of the law for those who, regardless of their status, have committed acts of criminal negligence and recklessness.

The worst and least desirable course of action would be senseless repression, which would constitute a regression to a time our country has left behind, such as what took place in '68, and what virtually happened over many years in countless cases of popular protests by farmers, workers, students and the urban and rural middle classes.

The prevailing and indeed growing climate of insecurity in certain regions of the country has damaged Mexico's image, and turned into an international scandal. The situation has been exacerbated by the lack of a clear strategy, with conclusive results, to prevent and counteract acts of violence and lead to those at the root of them to justice. The fact is most cases go unpunished, which hardly inspires confidence in the future of democracy, nor respect for the rule of law.

Those in government must not give up on working to establish negotiated agreements with every troubled section of society or environment, even if a consensus cannot be reached, because this is part of the democratic vision of civil responsibility. As problems accumulate, they should endeavour to adopt solutions that get to the bottom of each dispute, rather than just muddling through or banking on society remaining oblivious. That would be unforgiveable.

The serious and unresolved mining dispute, triggered by the immoral actions of a few powerful companies in 2006, with the active collusion of the last two PAN party governments, is a test of this current government's capacity and political will to overcome differences and finally resolve this conflict, by reaching a peace settlement with Mexico's most important political trade union of mining and metalworkers. The mistrust and doubts generated by anti-trade union corporations looking to impose their own interests at any cost must end now. Instead, they should be listening and responding to our proposal to build on a platform of modern, nationalist trade unionism for the 21st century.

The government must realise that these mounting disputes have to be tackled. There is the case of the Mexican Electricians Union (SME by its initials in Spanish), whose trade union integrity was damaged by the disappearance of the Luz y Fuerza del Centro company. Then there is the case of aviation workers, pilots and flight attendants alike, hit by the liquidation of the leading aeronautical company Mexicana de Aviación, which was simply so its owner Gastón Azcárraga, whose greed and lust for profits dragged the company into the ground, could escape justice.

Up to now, company bosses who commit crime or fraud have languished in complete impunity, such as in the cases of Oceanografía or Grupo México, with the horrendous levels of pollution and catastrophic environmental damage to the rivers, towns and residents of Cananea, Sonora; Taxco, Guerrero; and San Luis Potosí, among many others. In Grupo México's case, they are even still yet to be investigated and punished for the act of industrial homicide they committed at Pasta de Conchos coal mine in Coahuila, where 65 workers lost their lives. Not to mention Grupo Peñoles, and its cases of inhuman pollution and lead poisoning that have also gone unpunished, affecting children and residents of Torreón, Coahuila and Fresnillo, Zacatecas. The same goes for the fraud committed by Grupo Acerero del Norte's Alonso Ancira Elizondo, which has now been in suspension of payments for over ten years. The question is where have the law, justice and authority been in all of these cases?

Arising too, are many other old social conflicts from years ago back, with farmers, communal landowners, poor teachers and communities in mining areas, who view with real concern and protest not only the threats to their already chronically weakened social status, buried in pockets of humiliation and frustration, but also the fact that there are no long-term solutions.

There is no reason to expect that these voices will receive any adequate responses from politicians, and specifically from local authorities, which tend to play down the impact of these problems, using pretexts or excuses to absolve those responsible, arguments which would be inadmissible in a court of law.

Another burning issue that has not been properly tackled is the public insecurity resulting from the impact of criminal activity in the area of drug trafficking and kidnapping, carried out by groups which have emerged in response to weak government policy, purely to commit crime for personal gain. When Jesús Reyes Heroles warned years ago that we ought to be very careful about returning to the days of *México bronco* ('Wild Mexico'), he was referring to violent social protest and the outbreak of revolution in 1910, but today, *México bronco* is back in the form of organised crime, devastating entire populations.

The current explosion in protests about the Ayotzinapa or Tlatlaya cases demonstrate just how easily violence can find the government unprepared.

More intensive action on the part of government must be involved in rooting out the support that such criminal groups have from the public, business and finance sectors; so far, there has been no discernible impact of the government's decision to block their various overlapping sources of financial support. Such is the case with money laundering, which weaves itself throughout the fabric of society, with the financial authorities seemingly oblivious, still only interested in the large macroeconomic indicators that give the far from genuine impression of stability.

The state must undertake significant action to dismantle the build-up of conflicts, separating one from another to diminish their harmful cumulative effect. If we assume that tackling the lack of public security is crucial, which it is, other problems must be addressed, one by one, without reliance on some nonexistent respect for the law as a pretext. Doing so would draw a line under such illegal acts, both in the field of public safety as well as in the corporate and economic spheres.

This grave situation of public insecurity and impunity calls for an altered model of economic development, with a true commitment of political will to halt and put right the country's trajectory, and to open up new and improved opportunities for all Mexicans.

Economic Policy after the Elections

In Mexico, over the last three months, political parties and some civil, social, union and business organisations have been actively participating and speculating in the midterm elections for the Chamber of Deputies, on both federal and state level, as well as nine governorships of the states of the Republic that it was constitutionally necessary to elect.

Since the 7th of June, these same groups have turned to giving interpretations, opinions and information through the media about who won or lost in this electoral process, which has enthralled Mexican political activity, or at least did so previously. However, while this stage lasted many people forgot about what was happening with the application of an open and flexible commercial strategy that has been seriously dampening growth and the consolidation of national industry, through imports of certain subsidised and unregulated steel products, coming principally from China, Russia, Korea and Japan. This terrible effect on Mexican industrial development had already been denounced in some of the articles I wrote for La Jornada (Who is defending Mexico?, 2nd April 2015), as well as certain declarations and expositions published in various national newspapers on behalf of the National Union of Mine, Metal, Steel and Allied Workers of the Mexican Republic of which I have the honour of being President, in a mature and responsible approach to protecting sources of work.

However, they not only failed to offer solutions to the problem, but the country's situation became worse due to three fundamental factors:

1. The lack of a nationalist policy that is sensitive to the real needs of the economy and the population. The impression is that the government's most conservative forces have united their projects, their incapacity or their indifference in order to apply a blueprint of promotion and commercial relations totally at odds with national interests. Beyond this, they have put their submission to market laws and international agreements and conventions ahead of labour policy and general wellbeing, or worse still, ahead of the health, lives and happiness of Mexicans. In sum, they must be saying, the country and the majority of the population who live in increasing poverty can put up with it.

2. On the other hand we have the predatory, threatening, violent and denigrating attitude of some companies and businesspeople who have clearly demonstrated their opportunism and unchecked ambition to take advantage of the situation and begin to fire workers and make overblown or unjustified personnel adjustments, with no concern that these actions may further complicate the panorama of inequality and the critical problems associated, on the one hand, with organised delinquency or, on the other, social protest.

As such, in the area of mining, metalwork and steelwork a series of dismissals and technical stoppages of work were announced, which began to be applied at the end of March in the case of Arcelor Mittal, concerning over 900 non-unionised workers with the threat of reaching 2,000. Altos Hornos de México, owned by Alonso Ancira Elizondo, originally announced on the 26th of May a reduction of its workforce of 2,000 workers, which it later increased to 4,500 on the 3rd of June. At the same time, other companies, such as Grupo México, Grupo Peñoles, Grupo Industrial Monclova, Compañía Minera Autlán and many smaller ones, have joined this project to close down opportunities for dignified work for thousands of workers and their families and thus bury their hopes of achieving a decent or adequate standard of living for their future projects and that of their families. After all, who cares, apart from those affected, if profits come first with the privileged and dehumanised position in society. **Or perhaps they are the demons of unchecked and uncontrolled corruption and greed that are weakening industry to the extent of reducing it almost to a state of general coma. Where is the commitment of these companies towards the country?** Do politicians not realise that they could stop this terrible situation? Or do they not care?

3. The third related element, which goes hand in hand with or is a major part of this serious crisis, is the cynical attitude and total submission of many union leaders or pseudo-leaders who have capitulated and followed the orders of bosses to support them in their degrading betrayal. There are many cases in which they even support companies in the dismissal of staff, and in exchange for money they have handed over their conscience and other things to betray their own colleagues, whom they claim to represent.

What can happen under these circumstances? On the one hand, the government has taken certain actions to apply tariffs to some steel products imported at subsidised prices, without covering the wide range of industrial companies that would get some relief from this decision. Some company bosses have complained that these are improvised measures in the face of pressure, lacking any vision or use. Of course these very managers simultaneously cry and claim injury so as to increase the exploitation and control of the country's natural resources, demanding compensation and new concessions to keep or expand the privileges they have accumulated.

On the other hand, companies have introduced greater control over workers through blackmail, threats of dismissal, terror and submission in favour of their interests, with the use of *charros* and corrupt individuals, as well as pawns and thugs to avoid disagreements and rebellions.

At the same time, the control some of the most corrupt businessmen have over the media and dishonest journalists has increased dramatically, and they use them scrupulously on a daily basis to trick and lie to society about the real situation and their cloaked plans to commit abuses and greater exploitation of the country's workforce and natural resources. Fortunately, in the media there are some exceptions that lend dignity to life and the behaviour of society.

II. The Culture of Impunity

National Environmental Disaster

In addition to the massive exploitation of workers which so often goes hand in hand with the country's mining activity, we must consider the on-going environmental devastation in areas where minerals and metals are extracted or processed. This unregulated exploitation of natural resources is specifically due to the lack of government policies and regulations which should be in place to force mining and metalwork companies to comply with the conservation of water, soil, subsoil, forests, atmosphere, planta-tions, reedbeds, and pastures where biodiversity is being destroyed.

The activity of some mining and metalwork companies, which act without social responsibility, especially the most powerful among them, is closely linked with the irremediable damage done to ecosystems in min-ing areas. And if the companies very often do not offer basic conditions of security, industrial hygiene and health to their own workers, they care even less about protecting the environment. The fact is that, according to INEGI, the National Institute for Statistics and Geography, environmental damage costs the country 8 percent of its gross domestic product.

We don't have to go very far to see who is the principal culprit of this enormous environmental destruction. It is the federal government, for whom this is another failure on the list that it has been visibly accumu-lating in the two six-year terms of PAN (National Action Party) politics. The pillaging of the environment in mines and nearby areas is yet another product of short-sighted unilateral policymaking which only serves the in-terests of one sector: the mining companies. It is evident that the system is broken because the government never consults the people who live in villages surrounding the mining areas about the inevitable damage to the

71

local environment when it is handing out mining concessions to either Mexican or foreign companies. Above all when water supplies are abused in production processes and the cleaning of extracted material, contaminating it with cyanide and other chemical products, leaving communities without this basic resource. The government is at best criminally absent in this sphere, at worst complicit with and submissive to mining companies, from the moment the Ministry of the Economy gives mining land to the companies, without defining their limits or ensuring that companies have previously put in place stringent, binding promises to respect and preserve the environment. The search for profits determines the actions of businesses and government. Once more, ignorance and greed are put at the service of personal interests.

Under the two conservative governments which have been in power since 2000, mining concessions have been freely handed out, to such an extent that the two PAN administrations have given 26 percent of the national territory to Mexican and foreign-backed companies, and in recent years they have approved 757 foreign projects for mining extraction. This means that they have given mining groups approximately 56 million hectares of a total area of 200 million hectares over the whole country. The government gives a select few Mexican mining and metalwork companies concessions that are scandalously damaging to national interests, as in the case of Germán Larrea's Grupo México, which was recently awarded over 400 concessions, each one with over 15 thousand hectares, as well as the unconstitutional gratuity of the ability to exploit the methane gas which is released from coal mines. This was happening at the time of the industrial homicide at Pasta de Conchos in February 2006, which was this company's direct responsibility. None of these concessions has involved any serious environmental protection commitment, much less any respect for labour and human rights; no environmental protection went any further than being a written intention that was difficult to verify or never evaluated.

This has led communities in mining areas to protest bravely against environmental devastation, for reasons of simple survival or with regard to indigenous peoples' demand that their sacred areas be respected. The list of communities that have reacted against this situation is long, but the government gives them no way of voicing their concerns and no solution. As such we see how the mining company backed by Canadian capital, Minera San Xavier, which extracts gold and other minerals, has devastated Cerro San Pedro mine in San Luis Potosí, with the complicit support of federal and state governors, and where the participation of the ex-President Vicente Fox and his wife Martha Sahagún have been denounced as among the beneficiaries of this destruction, despite the protests of local people and a large sector of civil society. Similarly, faced with the endless stream of environmental violations, the federal government, as well as the governments of almost all the 26 states where there is mining activity, do no more than give vague promises and protracted explanations of the underlying problems. But then, instead of dealing with those problems, the use state security forces to crush community protests, just as they do with the labour demands of mine workers.

This is an incredibly serious emergency situation which should be placed at the top of the list of national priorities for the near future. **The way mining concessions are managed is completely idiotic and suicidal, and ignores environmental protection and conservation.** Mexico needs radical, firm policies against the squandering of non-renewable natural resources.

Industrial Homicide

February 19th, 2012 will mark six years since the tragedy which plunged the families of 65 miners into mourning, following a terrible explosion at the Pasta de Conchos coal mine in the municipality of San Juan de Sabinas, Coahuila. Six years since the "industrial homicide," as I called it at the time, committed by the company Grupo México and its president Germán Larrea, its board of directors led by Xavier García de Quevedo, and its administrative council. They forced miners to work in utterly unsafe and inhumane conditions, despite all the complaints filed, and the protests and strikes instigated by Los Mineros, our union that it is my honour to lead, which aimed to pressure Larrea y García de Quevedo into complying with their obligations as established in the collective labour contract (article 68); in the Federal Labour Law (article 132, section 17) and in the Political Constitution of the United Mexican States (article 123, section 14).

These have been six years of impunity, complicity and protection for Larrea and Grupo México on the part of Vicente Fox's and Felipe Calderón's governments. None of the three –Larrea, Fox or Calderón– visited the mine to give their condolences to the families and much less to offer the technical, material and financial support that was required to rescue the miners, leaving their families helpless.

Beyond this, on the fifth day after the explosion, the chemical engineer and supplier of Grupo México in its private companies in San Luis Potosí, Francisco Javier Salazar, who Fox named Secretary of Labour, along with the Grupo México administrators led by the submissive García de Quevedo, hurriedly closed and sealed the mine, ordered the Army to stop their rescue efforts, and then like true cowards they all left the area.

Those people were totally insensitive and perversely irresponsible: they abandoned the miners without knowing whether they were still alive and without listening to the protests, the deep hurt and the anger of the families and the Los Mineros union in the face of that heartless decision. The miners were left at a depth of only 120 metres, where the bodies of 63 of them still lie today. They wanted to prevent anyone finding out the cause of the explosion and collapse in the mine or the awful safety conditions and the lack of health and hygiene that prevailed, products of the complicit irresponsibility which stems from the shared corruption of authorities and businessmen.

In order to put the miserable behaviour of Larrea and Grupo México into focus, we must return to Chile in 2010 where, under a conservative government like the one that is currently in power in Mexico, a successful operation ensured the rescue of 33 miners after they were buried alive following an explosion and collapse on 5 August at the San José de Atacama mine near San José de Copiapó. The area is mountainous and the miners were 700 metres down under hard rock, as opposed to the soft, flat terrain of Pasta de Conchos. The miners there were found alive on the 17th day after rescue efforts began, as opposed to in Pasta de Conchos when the miners were abandoned on the fifth day after the tragedy and thus condemned to death. The political persecution of Mexican union leaders based on false accusations began immediately after this. Larrea's Grupo México and Vicente Fox's government conspired to create a smokescreen that would divert attention away from their serious criminal negligence, but the rescue in Chile exposed them to the world.

In Chile, the successful rescue mission lasted 69 days, but the same approach was not taken in Mexico. Another aspect further illustrates the meanness of Larrea and his partners: in Chile they negotiated compensation of almost one million dollars per worker, while in Pasta de Conchos each family was offered a miserable and humiliating 75,000 pesos, equivalent to around $7,000 dollars. In contrast, in the Upper Big Ranch coal mine in West Virginia, United States, where there was an explosion in April 2010 and 29 miners were killed, President Barack Obama visited the site of the tragedy several times and each family received $3 million dollars in compensation.

Germán Larrea and his partners and associates are like bodies without souls, they have no principles, no sense of guilt and much less any sense of personal, social, civil or legal responsibility for their actions. Human life has no value for them.

As a result of this national and international disgrace, powerful international union organisations have agreed to carry out, from 19 to 25 February this year, intense days of action that will be more forceful than those of 2011, to denounce Felipe Calderón's government for its inaction, its repression and its violations of the International Agreements on respecting the Right to Organise, Autonomy and Freedom of Association. The arguments are self-evident: the situation of workers in Mexico has deteriorated, the abusive protection contracts systems have spread further, the physical and legal intimidation and the psychological torture of workers has intensified, with corporations and government acting in complicity with one another.

The world is watching them and has condemned them. International union organisations are mobilising with acts of protest at Mexican embassies and consulates and they are writing letters to Felipe Calderón to pressure him to stop this aggression and to respect labour and human rights. If no change is made, the actions will escalate until abuses of power, corruption and constant violations of the rule of law are stopped. Those businessmen, the National Action Party and Calderón must immediately set right their actions against the Mexican people, before their time runs out and the condemnation of them is sustained permanently until it brings them to justice.

Blood Mines

Traditionally, the development of mining and the metal transformation industry has been linked in Mexico to the uncontrolled exploitation of mineral resources and the workforce. This situation, however, has intensified during the last 12 years due to the lack of a rational policy of respect for human rights, from which our country is straying further and further.

The unchecked ambition of some businesspeople and the complicity of municipal, state and federal governments has brought on this terrible progression. There are more work accidents in mines and processing plants than there were twelve years ago. **Inhuman conditions are increasingly prevalent, to the point that they are turning the industrial activity of this important sector into frequent acts of corporate terrorism** against the labour and human rights of both workers and the population at large.

There are clear and obvious cases of cover ups and official protection of certain companies, which given the government's servility is deplorable as well as dishonest. This miserable, shameless role has been played by the Ministers for Work, Francisco Javier Salazar under Vicente Fox, and Javier Lozano Alarcón under Felipe Calderón. This breed of bureaucrats have corrupted this ministry's responsibility, they have turned it into a booty to be plundered by a few while most of the country's workers and democratic independent unions are suppressed. Today both men, supported by the PAN (National Action Party) and by the businesspeople who have abjectly served it, are attempting to take up positions in the Senate, from where, if they get there, they will continue to betray and harm the country, drawing up and changing laws so as to cynically serve their bosses better.

Meanwhile, workers continue to be exploited. Grupo Peñoles has had, over the last two years, over 20 deaths and 40 serious injuries in its mines and processing plants. It has also used groups of paramilitaries, traitors and thugs when workers have protested, as was the case when the mine worker Juventino Flores Salas was beaten to death with pipes and spades Fresnillo, Zacatecas on the 10th June 2009. Others were also seriously injured and vehicles were destroyed, and no authority has stepped in when these crimes are officially investigated.

Peñoles has also spent many years contaminating the environment and water supplies with lead, zinc and other metals which do irreversible damage to the health of hundreds of children, whole communities and the workers themselves in plants in Torreón, Coahuila and other regions of Mexico.

Grupo Acerero del Norte, GAN, has committed similar or worse crimes in Monclova and in the coal-mining region of Coahuila, without any state or federal government investigating or sanctioning it with the full weight of the law. As well as repressing and using thugs to control and humiliate workers and to impose protection contracts, GAN directors have devoted themselves to corrupting a clique of traitors to disassociate workers from their union organisation, to mutilate collective contracts and to hand over the rights and victories accumulated over 60 years to sham unions, in blatant complicity with the CTM (the Confederation of Mexican Workers) and Coahuila state governments. Without a doubt they are preparing the ground to hand over the company to their Korean associates in the Pohang Iron and Steel Company, at the expense of their own workers and the blood they spill.

Of course the pinnacle of corruption and cynicism is Grupo México, which is counted among the world's 10 least ethical companies because it never protects peoples' lives or their health. Wherever it operates, it always carries destruction and death, as in the case of its subsidiary the Southern Peru Copper Corporation, based in Peru, or its ex-parent company the American Smelting and Refining Company, Asarco, based in the United States. It has also demonstrated its cynical attitude at Pasta de Conchos and the other mines and units which it exploits in Mexico and abroad.

From 2006 until the date on which the shareholders and the board of directors of Grupo México decided to attack the miners' union, they have had over 100 deaths and 200 injuries among miners. In Cananea alone, since the 6th June 2010, when they illegally occupied the mine after an obvious legal pretence with the full backing of the government and over 4 thousand members of the PFP (the Federal Preventive Police), the state police and even the Army, over 20 untrained contractors have died and there have been over 100 injuries, not only among the strike-breakers who are recruited from as far away as Central America but also among members of the police forces themselves.

Grupo México, alongside Peñoles and GAN, have turned their mines and plants into true concentration camps where they systematically repress, torture and humiliate workers; it is a form of disguised modern slavery. Elsewhere, they dazzle the PAN government with new sums of additional investments. Through this over-exploitation of human labour and an unprecedented growth of the mining sector, Germán Larrea, of Grupo México and Alberto Bailleres, of Peñoles, have become the second and third richest men in Mexico, according to *Forbes*.

We must put a stop to the brutal exploitation in these blood mines, as they are known the world over. The next government has the moral, social and legal obligation to stop and to put right this absurd policy of the irrational exploitation of the workforce and of human beings. It must also put in place a law, as I have been suggesting, that punishes companies' irresponsibility and criminal negligence.

Unethical Companies

It is regrettable, shameful and contemptible that so many Mexican companies act without any kind of social responsibility, and are among the least ethical operators in the world of business. Yet they claim to be exemplary, alleging that they comply with legal and moral standards. In flagrant attacks on the information gathered in Mexico and across the world about their social irresponsibility, which only the current conservative government fails to notice, and even rewards, these companies have been publicly patting themselves on the back and thus confirming their evident lack of ethics by boasting about morals they do not possess.

These companies are Grupo México, owned by Germán Feliciano Larrea Mota Velasco, and Grupo Villacero, which belongs to the brothers Julio, Sergio y Pablo Villarreal Guajardo who hail from Matamoros, Tamaulipas. Both companies have been advertising, in the press and other media, the fact that they have received awards, one from Concamin (the Confederation of Industrial Chambers), on the February 28, and the other from an association in London, on the February 29. The Concamin award is named 'Ethics and values in industry'.

Worst of all is that in the case of Grupo México, the president himself Felipe Calderón rushed to Guadalajara to present the company with the Concamin award, making it clear, once more, that there is an unlawful complicity between them.

On this matter, the Geneva-based Covalence, an independent consulting firm which analyses the ethical indices of companies, published a report on 26 January which placed Grupo México among the least ethical companies in the world. It was ranked 573rd out of a total of 586 corporations that were assessed, and in the natural resources sector, it was ranked 31 out of 32.

Larrea Mota Velasco's Grupo México stands out because of its insulting profit margins in recent years which are due, among other things, to the company's cruel repression of employees and their fair labour demands as well as its criminal insensitivity towards the lives and security of its workers: this was demonstrated by the industrial homicide at Pasta de Conchos, Coahuila, in February 2006. The bodies of 63 of the 65 miners who died there have still not been recovered. This is a real **national disgrace and its perpetrators, the company's owner, partners and directors, have still not received the punishment they deserve.** The widows and families of the miners who were killed have received nothing but contempt and persecution from Larrea, in an eloquent expression of the ethics that he uses in his company. But thanks to all this, Larrea is the second richest man in Mexico according to *Forbes*.

This corporation also stands out due to its lack of ethics and its inhuman refusal to resolve, through legal channels, the three legitimate strikes in Cananea, Sonora; Sombrerete, Zacatecas, and Taxco, Guerrero, which have now been running for around five years. To this we must add the complicity of Felipe Calderón's government which sent over four thousand members of federal and state police forces into Cananea on 6 June 2010. This came after the illegal attempt to terminate labour relations at that mine, but where they have resumed rehabilitation work, violating the legal norm, which states that in a legitimate strike, as is the case there, the contracting of new workers or resuming of any kind of productive activity is not permitted.

In this case, Grupo México has contracted several thousand third parties or strikebreakers since that police offensive, without having offered them any training. Those people are kept in conditions of inhumane slavery, working in virtual concentration camps, threatened and humiliated every day by armed men who guard their every movement. 20 people have been killed and over 100 injured at this mine due to the company's negligence, which is always concealed. The third party workers live like slaves under the control of a *charro* leader, Javier Villarreal, and the local CTM (Confederation of Mexican Workers) is complicit in this.

Another serious case of murder by Grupo México's paramilitaries took place in Nacozari, Sonora, on August 11, 2007. A worker named Reynaldo Hernández González was shot to death by these guards, and 20 of his co-workers were tortured; they were on their way back to work after an award was rendered in their favour. Those who orchestrated and carried out the attack remain unpunished, protected by all the ethics that Larrea and his partners can muster, which is rewarded by Calderón and Concamin.

As for the Villarreal Guajardo brothers' Grupo Villacero, on 20 April 2006 this company sparked the repression by federal and state forces of the legal strike led by workers at the industrial port of Lázaro Cárdenas, Michoacán. On that day Mario Alberto Castillo and Héctor Álvarez Gómez were murdered, and more than 100 workers were seriously injured. It is also public knowledge that the Villarreal Guajardo brothers previously admitted that they were the main cause of the bankruptcy of Fundidora de Fierro y Acero de Monterrey, declared on May 10, 1986.

These are the two cases of businessmen, Larrea Mota Velasco and the Villarreal Guajardo brothers, who are desperately buying, at any cost, the pedigree that they altogether lack, in order to boast that they are the most ethical and socially responsible. **And Calderón gives them all the recognition that they do not deserve, ignoring international condemnation, instead of making them pay for their disgraceful crimes.**

Bodies without Souls

As everyone knows, on April 11 nine workers who had been trapped for a week by a collapse in the Cabeza de Negro mine, in the Ica region of Peru, were rescued with full participation from the government. The effort was led by the president himself, Ollanta Humala, followed by his colleagues as well as the union and the mining population.

In my article published on April 12, 2012 I wrote: "A rescue in Peru, another embarrassment for the Mexican government. I am in no doubt that when the will and a sense of responsibility exist, objectives can be reached. This successful effort in Peru, similar to that in San José de Copiapó, Chile, make patently clear the full extent of the human misery caused by Grupo México in Pasta de Conchos when it abandoned 65 of its workers in that 'industrial homicide' which will always be associated with Germán Larrea, Vicente Fox, Francisco Javier Salazar, Felipe Calderón, Javier Lozano Alarcón, Fernando Gómez Mont and other collaborators, accomplices, directors and shareholders of this company who have no ethical standards or respect for human life."

Two weeks later, I stand by what I said and I wish to expand upon it. **Those who are responsible and who I named acted not only without any moral or ethical standards, they also showed how little human life means to them, even the lives of those workers whose hard work and sacrifice make those businessmen richer**, especially Germán Feliciano Larrea Mota Velasco who Mexican miners, and workers the world over, rightfully call an unpunished murderer of miners. This man continues to rely on the despicable complicity of Vicente Fox and Felipe Calderón as well as the aforementioned ministers in their governments, in order to hide the true causes of this tragedy which according to all the evidence is the result of Grupo México's criminal negligence and irresponsibility in not installing adequate industrial health, safety and hygiene measures to preserve the wellbeing and lives of miners.

This is a matter which cannot be forgotten nor left to go unpunished. Above all because Grupo México not only left those men to die when they closed the mine only five days after the Pasta de Conchos collapse, but also because since then they have offered only the meanest compensation to the families and relatives of the 65 miners who lost their lives on 19 February 2006. Furthermore, the company has used repressive state and federal forces to persecute, as if they were common criminals, the widows and families who are clamouring for their rights to be respected and for the bodies of their husbands, brothers or sons to be recovered in order to give them a decent burial.

Larrea's Grupo México and Fox and Calderón's governments have played leading roles in a story of horror, disgrace and injustice. It is not enough that the second of these leaders is soon to relinquish his presidential power, the legitimacy of which has been questioned during this term, nor that the first has already left office. If all these guilty parties remain unpunished, particularly Francisco Javier Salazar and Javier Lozano Alarcón, Ministers of Labour in the two respective governments, Mexican society will be left with the open wound of this great injustice, which should be punished by law and thus serve as an example.

Criminal negligence should never again be permitted in any company, mining or otherwise, in Mexico. For this reason I have called for legislation that punishes the people who are guilty of these corporate murders, as they are called the world over, and puts them behind bars. It is not acceptable that the perpetrators of such tragedies are left in perfect freedom while grief swamps the families of the dead miners, families who have lost their main breadwinner and who, on top of that, have been crushed and treated as delinquents.

In contrast, on April 5, 2010 when there was an accident at the Upper Big Branch coal mine in West Virginia, United States, President Barack Obama himself visited the area on two occasions to be with the families of 29 workers who were killed. After those visits, Obama spearheaded the effort to legislate against irresponsibility in his country so that such a tragedy would never happen again. Additionally, this pressure served to ensure that the families of those who died received compensation of 3 million dollars each, as opposed to the miserable $7,000 which Grupo México, with government approval, proposed to give to each family from Pasta de Conchos.

The lesson from the recent incident at the Cabeza de Negro mine in Ica, Peru, is to show the shamelessness of Germán Larrea's Grupo México: the company has continued its immoral attacks on workers and their union at every available opportunity. This is clearly shown by the exploitation of strike breakers at the mine at Cananea, Sonora, which it turned into a true concentration camp, just as it intends to do in Sombrerete, Zacatecas and Taxco, Guerrero, where workers are striking heroically. Mexican society can no longer allow businessmen to arrogantly and ignorantly disregard the lives of workers, with an utter lack of social responsibility or human sensibility, nor to go through life as they truly are, bodies without souls.

Agents of Change

12 years ago, in 2000, when the PAN (National Action Party) came to power, all Mexicans asked themselves if in that election they had made the right decision for the future of Mexico, having lived through a period of inefficiency and arrogance under the PRI (Industrial Revolutionary Party) government.

Now, 12 years later, the major error that we made in electing a conservative, reactionary party full of incompetent, mediocre corrupt politicians with no social, legal or moral sensitivity is blatantly clear.

Mexico is currently experiencing one of the worst periods in its history. Widespread corruption, neglect of the population's problems and needs, rising unemployment, both open and hidden, with 14 million people out of work, and an absurd war on organised crime that lacks strategy, vision and alternatives, is condemned to failure, and has meant the death or disappearance of over 150 thousand people.

It is now clearer than ever that Vicente Fox Quesada, Felipe Calderón Hinojosa and their accomplices and collaborators never had an adequate strategy or any nationalist interest in putting Mexico and Mexicans first.

For them it is simply a case of unreservedly handing over the country's natural resources, since today over 25 per cent of the country has been given away in concessions to mining companies and the extractive industry who monopolise and speculate with land to their own ends. **The servile appeasement of foreign and national business interests and the loss of sovereignty mean nothing to these governments.** What is more, they believe and are convinced that they have acted correctly. They have no shame, but this does not bother them, and they try to convince the population by using the media to contaminate the minds of Mexicans.

The cynicism that prevails in government prevents them from seeing that they themselves are the origin and the centre of the wrongs of these past 12 years, with their boundless personal ambition and their lack of principles and values. Even more importantly, however, is the constant violation of the rule of law and the perversion in the application of justice for their benefit and that of the people who act in complicity with them, businesspeople, reactionaries, unethical media, unscrupulous politicians and all the flora and fauna of corruption. As a consequence, we now see the destruction of the national system, as well as the negation of a future filled with hope, justice, dignity and happiness for current and future generations.

But today, thousands, even millions of students and young people who are prepared and conscious, who have woken up and are disillusioned with the current situation, have denounced these abuses that have built up over time. Their expression of dissatisfaction has coincided with that of the unions and free workers who have been fighting for democracy for many years and demanding an end to the impunity surrounding the serious and profound violations committed by governments in the last 30 years.

This new movement of young people in society must grow stronger every day, demanding a radical move away from this economic and social model that exploits the population and our country's natural resources.

They can certainly count on the unconditional solidarity of the majority of independent, democratic and respectable intellectuals and journalists, of the working class in rural areas, in industry and in services, of honest politicians and businesspeople in Mexico and abroad. Nonetheless, they must absolutely not lose their drive, enthusiasm and true desire for change and transformation towards a fairer, safer, freer and more democratic society.

Together, we and those young people are the new actors and agents of change. Let us not lose the drive or the opportunity so that in six years, if we get there peacefully, we will not feel the same regret of not having correctly chosen the government that we need. Let there be no repetition of the negative and contemptuous statement that the people gets the government it deserves; that is an insult to the intelligence and the moral and human integrity of the Mexican people.

Young people burst onto the public scene when they quickly deduced from the positions of the political parties in power and their allies that those people saw the electoral process as a simple exercise that would conclude with the announcement of their supposed victory. Their enthusiastic participation is a warning that this will not be the case, because students are demonstrating strong morals and values that have not been seen for years, which must be used to build an element of fundamental stimulus for all social and political forces, and for the members of society who long for substantial change.

Listening attentively and calmly to the call of young people is, right now, a priority for the whole country, so that we might obtain the results proposed by this sensitive sector of Mexican society. They want no more blood to be spilled, no more violations of the rule of law, no more attacks on their own future and the future of all Mexicans.

Pasta de Conchos: An Historic Disgrace

Today marks seven years of impunity, neglect and aggression from Grupo México towards the 65 workers who died in mine 8 at Pasta de Conchos, in the municipality of San Juan de Sabinas, Coahuila. This tragedy has shown the obvious complicity and corruption of politicians and bureaucrats in covering up a clear case of criminal negligence by Germán Feliciano Larrea Mota Velasco and his company, who have behaved with complete depravity, irresponsibility and indifference.

The world remembers the success of Chilean miners in 2010, when they rescued 33 workers who had been buried alive 750 metres underground in San José de Copiapó, 69 days after there was a collapse in the mine. In Mexico we cannot forget the anger and sadness when the explosion took place in the Pasta de Conchos coal mine, where Grupo México, Vicente Fox and Larrea abandoned the 65 workers who were trapped at a depth of only 120 metres, on the fifth day of a simulated rescue attempt. Fox, Francisco Javier Salazar, then Secretary of Labour, and above all Germán Larrea, decided to close the mine without knowing whether the miners were alive. They had the sole intention of hiding the causes of the tragedy, that is to say, the criminal negligence, arrogance and irresponsibility with which Grupo México, it directors, partners and accomplices have acted and remained in the shadows.

The industrial homicide that was committed there has still not been investigated and those responsible have not been punished. It is an historic disgrace that the union has denounced on many occasions and which must not be allowed to continue, because it damages the image of Mexico and reveals an absurd illegal system of protection which denigrates the Mexican justice system. A country with no rule of law is a country with no future, heading for failure. The absurdity is that over the last seven years Mexico has been commanding less and less respect on the political and legal world stage, only to protect a small group of businessmen led by Larrea who do not value or respect the life or health of their employees and workers.

The depressing role of depravity, abuse and corruption in this inner circle has imposed something entirely undue on Mexico and its people. This group's cowardice cannot represent or transmit the image of a nation that in the overwhelming majority is made up of decent people. The working class and their families are waiting for the current government to announce the start of the work of recovering the abandoned bodies, 63 of which are buried in the mine. They are waiting for an investigation to be opened up to determine the causes of the disaster and punish those responsible at whatever level, and to force Grupo México to fairly compensate the families of the miners who died in this terrible and denigrating crime.

Today we must remember that neither Germán Larrea, nor the ex-presidents Vicente Fox and Felipe Calderón, ever visited the mine to give instructions or assure that the rescue was going ahead, not even to give their condolences and the necessary support for those affected by the explosion, which was a product of cowardice, ambition, arrogance and criminal negligence.

The current government would not only distance itself from the cowardice of those shady characters but would also grow massively in terms of political prestige and as an administration that guarantees human rights. Today, the 19th of February, is the seventh anniversary of these shameful and unforgettable events, and Larrea and Grupo México' shareholders, directors, partners and accomplices, who include the ex-president, must be hiding so as not to show the cynicism and shame that they will wear forevermore. Up to now, nothing and no one has made them react because they feel protected and like the lords of the corrupt fantasy world into which they have turned our great country. On the contrary, they have been allowed to hide in plain sight with impunity, buying off journalists and manipulating the media, mercenary judges, and commerce organizations, like those for mining and steelwork. Politicians and ex-workers have sold out and submitted to their interests in the most vulgar and cheap way possible. As such, our dignity has been lost because unscrupulous people have been used to pervert and deform reality and justice, promoting false and slanderous public attacks that lack all decency and ethics.

They should apologise and give explanations to the families, the miners' union, the Mexican people and the wider world, which is constantly watching. Today's government must set an example of honour and morals by ensuring that justice is done at Pasta de Conchos, whoever it might bring down. No one can or should be above the law, however powerful they seem or believe themselves to be, however many false investments they announce in their favour to impress superficial politicians, without revealing the high human and social costs, the indiscriminate exploitation of natural resources, the contamination of towns and communities, tax evasion and the persistence of a system of privilege and impunity, which has worn on the souls of millions of decent, honest and hard-working Mexican people.

The corruption, cynicism and demented behaviour of Larrea and his associates know no limits, except the strength of those of us who are fighting for justice to be done and the rule of law to be correctly applied by the Mexican State.

Rescued in Chile, abandoned in Mexico. A permanent disgrace that the people responsible will always carry on their consciences, which are stained with the blood of miners. This industrial homicide, as I called it at the time and which is now openly recognised as such, should never have happened and must never be repeated. That is why we need a dignified example through the correct, good faith application of the law, for the good of education and the principles and values of current and future generations.

The Cowards are Scared

On Thursday 2nd May I wrote, in a public declaration: "When it comes to justice, Mexico is a country of chiaroscuros. There are great and brave judges like Jesús Terríquez and Manuel Bárcena, and there are others like Núñez Sandoval who dishonour the legal profession and make spiteful, illegal judgements, as well as climbing through the ranks thanks to friends and favours but also by trampling the rights of those below them. This man, Luis Núñez Sandoval, puts the justice that he should be representing and administrating to shame, shielding himself, it is said, with protection that, he states, "comes from an ex-senior legal civil servant."

This quote refers to the fact that while two judges, Jesús Terríquez y Manuel Bárcena, basing their decisions on the spirit and the letter of the respective law, had rightly authorised my protection against the latest false accusation aimed at me in the previously terminated and resolved matter of the mining trust. The other aforementioned judge, Núñez Sandoval, who took over from judge Bárcena, reversed his colleague's decision, arguing that he is not Bárcena and does not have to think or act like him. This is evidently ridiculous because both acted in the same tribunal, Bárcena in one way, with the correct application of the law, and Núñez Sandoval in the opposite way, contradicting the law.

What the negative Núñez Sandoval said is truly pathetic because it is comparable to the president of the Republic annulling the previous president's acts with one stroke of his pen and pointing out the fact that he doesn't think like his predecessor. **The institution is the same, with one or with the other, it doesn't matter who leads it.**

In reality, Núñez Sandoval was promoted before the Judiciary Council by one of the offices of the country's biggest power brokers, at the service of Grupo México, made up of Fernando Gómez Mont, Julio Esponda and Alberto Zínser, as well as lawyers of much lower calibre but who are mercenaries equally lacking in ethical standards such as Agustín Acosta Azcón who uses fake company names such as Veta de Plata. These people also carry the genes of wickedness, perversity, and corruption inherited from their progenitors.

I mention this subject because as my pursuers are running out of possibilities to attack me through legal tribunals – thanks to the sound legal defence that has carried my case forward – so their false accusations get worse. They invent renewed arrest warrants that contradict the verdicts given on 11 occasions by the tribunals exonerating me as union leader, stating that I have acted within the law, honestly and transparently with regard to our organisation. These verdicts frustrate the morbid desires of the enemies of the miners' union, and they bring forward the date of my return to Mexico. This is what motivates their fear and cowardice. They know that my return to Mexico, with the due guarantees of physical and legal security, means that their seven years of political persecution will have been reduced to nothing, it will have been a sterile effort, and that I will be able to act in favour of democracy and the freedom of association of my mining colleagues and the Mexican working class.

In this way Germán Feliciano Larrea and other businessmen in the mining sector desperately and feverishly use their frontmen or nominees, such as the aforementioned offices, to give the impression that I still have unresolved legal issues regarding the mining trust. They obsessively return time and again to the tired, false idea that up to 55 million dollars were supposedly siphoned out of said trust belonging to the mining union, when from the outset, in 1990, an insolvency judge stated – and Germán Larrea accepted this – that those funds belong to the National Miners' Union, Los Mineros, and that the union could use them according to its own decisions. Parallel audits showed that not a single cent has been diverted from those amounts, a proportion of which are now frozen by banks following the illegal and unjust ruling by the PAN government, but there they are and, with the union's exclusive agreement, the rest of said funds have already been handed over to the miners whose right it was to receive a share.

These last few days have been plagued with gossip about my legal situation, and it is patently evident that, faced with my return to Mexico, there is fear or rather panic **among the arrogant and immoral businessmen who have pursued me politically and legally** with the complicity of the two previous PAN governments – bad experiences that must not be repeated under the current government of Enrique Peña Nieto – **there is fear, or rather sheer panic, about my return to Mexico**. Above all there is total cowardice in the face of the fact that they are being beaten in their plans to put an end to my leadership and to the National Miners' union, Los Mineros, which shows itself to be stronger and more united than ever despite these seven hard years of conflict.

Many lawyers, judges, magistrates and even ministers of the Court have played a positive role in preventing abuses of power and corruption, as well as the legal blasphemy which would find the leaders of the miners' union guilty.

That is why in the declaration mentioned at the beginning of this article, I noted that: The Federal Justice Council and the Supreme Court of Justice have gone to great lengths to achieve an excellent administration of justice. There still is much to do. One starting point is to thoroughly revise cases such as that of Núñez Sandoval, which do so much damage to the image of Judicial Power, so as to change, to correct and to get to the bottom of things. **In this way we would honour all those many noble judges who do their jobs every day with true vocation, impartiality, respect for the law and honesty.** This is how it should be.

Threats and Blackmail against Mexico

Improvisation, incompetent government, stupidity, arrogance and corruption led to a failed economic policy for the 12 years of Vicente Fox and Felipe Calderón's PAN governments, commonly referred to as the tragic dozen. They led to truly disastrous consequences in certain sectors of industry, trade and services. In fact, for every nine businesses established in 2009, only two survived in 2012, with many companies consequently facing economic and social collapse.

The body that provided these figures is the National Institute of Statistics and Geography (INEGI, by its initials in Spanish), arising from the first Demographic Study of Businesses conducted in its important history. A total of 968,000 SMEs (small and medium sized enterprises), each employing up to 100 workers, disappeared over this period. That is to say that the great majority of companies that went into liquidation are those that have contributed 90 percent of formal jobs to the national economy, and are therefore considered key to the development and growth of productive activity.

The most frustrating thing is the depression and desperation that this has generated for many Mexicans, undoubtedly bright people, with original and novel ideas, who genuinely believed in their projects, efforts, energy, their spirit of self-improvement and in helping to generate more opportunities for themselves, their families and for Mexico.

Many of these people decided to leave for abroad or were left obliged by the situation to join the informal economy. The PRI government hasn't been able to overcome this disastrous inheritance and nor has it managed to find a clean way out in the face of such national disappointment and injustice.

103

By contrast, the governments of the two previous administrations dedicated themselves to protecting big business and consortia, at the expense of the frustrated programmes to promote small and medium sized start-ups. They either forgot, or simply didn't care, that it is these companies that generate the largest volume of jobs, increasing revenue and purchasing power, which in turn stimulate demand and overall economic growth.

Today, the same monopolies and corporations that received all the aid, concessions and resources from Fox and Calderón, are pressurising and blackmailing the current government into cancelling or withdrawing reforms that do not suit their interests, such as the tax reform and the tax deduction from the profits of the wealthiest. They show approval instead for other reforms that open up new and improved opportunities for investment and increasing their wealth ever more rapidly and at any cost, even denationalisation, as in the proposed energy reform.

In truth it is double speak and hypocrisy on the part of those business groups, a lack of loyalty, patriotism and respect for the nation, which attests to their disdain for Mexico and the Mexican people.

Society is seeing how, despite the benefits obtained from the country's governments and resources, the largest companies in terms of size are engaged in a raging media and lobbying battle with the judiciary to prevent the treasury reform from being passed, which is set to place a levy on those who have the most and to redress a cause of profound economic imbalance, namely the very low tax contributions made by large consortia. They are currently placing pressure and blackmailing the government, by confronting it and legislators with the direct challenge of withdrawing investment and leaving the country, or by making the argument that these new taxes – which are certainly paid anywhere else – prevent them from being competitive, which is patently false.

Grupo México, led by Germán Feliciano Larrea Mota Velasco, is a clear example of those companies that saw the most benefit from liberal economic policy and then went on to grow and become monstrous conglomerations of power and monopoly, whose holdings even include mining companies, cinema chains, thoroughbred horses and railways formerly under state ownership; they manufacture televisions, own airports and have myriad other business interests. **Today, this conglomerate is undertaking an obsessive assault on the very government that has given them everything, and opposes any organisation, person or trade union that defends itself through legal channels, while repeatedly violating the rule of law itself.**

If Grupo México does indeed want to leave the country, an argument it uses as a threat, then let it head for London, England, accompanied by its entire Board of Directors, its managers, its 30 offices of influence-peddling lawyers and its media cronies. Justice is waiting for Larrea there, to hold him criminally accountable for the major fraud committed against English investors. Around 10 years ago he sold them over 70 million dollars in shares, valued today at roughly 2 billion dollars, but which he characteristically hasn't handed over to date, just as he did, for example, with the National Union of Miners or the shareholders of the Southern Perú Copper Corporation. Let's see if Larrea is capable of making his case in a public hearing before the courts there in London and can stop hiding away, despite the fact that he doesn't even deign to attend social events hosted by other companies here in Mexico. What is he so afraid of that he has to hide?

The Struggle Continues

Last week, the 30th of July, marks seven years to the day since three miners' strikes broke out, heroic struggles for the justice, respect and dignity of more than two thousand workers in the mines of Cananea, Sonora as well as Taxco, Guerrero and San Martín Sombrerete, Zacatecas. These movements for improved working conditions, health, safety, hygiene and a better standard of living for families are some of the longest disputes, if not the longest, in the history of the workers' movement and social struggles in Mexico.

The state concession granted for these mines is held by the most arrogant and dehumanising company in the country, none other than Germán Feliciano Larrea's Grupo México, the very same company that caused the death of 65 workers at the Pasta de Conchos coal mine, in San Juan de Sabinas, Coahuila on 19th February 2006. Right up to today, 63 bodies remain abandoned 120 metres beneath the earth thanks to the heartlessness of the company, its shareholders and directors, combined with the indifference of the two previous PAN party governments and the current ruling PRI government.

Neither political party cares about the families' suffering, the constant calls and demands from the National Miners Union, Lost Mineros, which I am honoured to lead, nor the requests from international bodies like the International Labour Organisation (ILO), IndustriALL Global Union and even Interpol, to bring an end to the impunity and shame of having abandoned workers whose effort and sacrifice over many years helped to generate the wealth of this and other heartless and criminal companies,

companies which have received and continued to receive privileges and great tracts of land that rightfully belong to the nation.

It seems that we have reached such heights of cynicism and corruption in Mexico that people no longer care about a tragedy, unless they are the ones who have suffered and experienced it in their own lives. How is it possible that patent acts of criminal negligence by companies like Germán Larrea's Grupo México, Alberto Bailleres González's Peñoles, and Alonso Ancira Elizondo's Grupo Acerero del Norte continue to be protected and covered up, when globally they are categorised and defined as some of the least ethical corporations on the planet, existing and functioning solely for profit and at the expense of the life and health of their own workers.

Those mining lords and barons who perennially want to appear on the world's rich lists, are the very same who exploit mines and industrial plants systems of slavery and like veritable concentration camps, constantly riding roughshod over workers' rights. **Nevertheless, the dignity of workers transcends, and will always transcend, their corruption and greed.**

What is worse, however, is that they continue to receive concessions of land, resources and new financial privileges. The question that we Mexicans are asking ourselves is, whose hands are we in, given that these companies are completely unmoved by the suffering of thousands of families at Pasta de Conchos and in the three mines which have now been on strike for seven long years? The situation is both absurd and negligent. The bodies of the fallen miners are not being rescued, meaning the parties guilty of committing serious criminal negligence remain free from punishment, and until now free from resolving the three labour strikes, which have continued for seven years since they were first triggered by Grupo México.

Another question: Is there not a single person in government with enough sensitivity and humanity to prevent and resolve these acts of abuse? Lest we forget that a government which fails to respect the rule of law and justice is a government on course for disaster and social breakdown.

Today it is of the utmost importance and urgency to oblige Grupo México and every other company to respect collective bargaining agreements and to sit down to negotiate a solution to the three strikes, as well as to put forward a plan for the immediate recovery of the bodies of the sacrificed miners. **They go around preaching that the stability and peace of Mexico's labour market offer a model for other nations across the globe. Do they really expect to be listened to and heeded, given the prevailing reality of the situation in Mexico?**

There has to be a limit to the manipulation and lies, and if we want to regain respect for Mexico's significantly tarnished image in the outside world. This is becoming increasingly urgent and necessary. Consistent and moderate action will be required if we are to get to the bottom of the national problems and troubles that dash the hopes of our people.

This is why we need to resolve these strikes within the law and with complete respect for fundamental workers' rights, whether they be mining and metalworkers, or involved in any other industry related to the transformation and manufacture of metal and steel. The authorities must act immediately to bring an end to these disputes, the three strikes and the rescue of the human souls abandoned at Pasta de Conchos. There is no room for indifference from the government or the politicians and businessmen responsible, not in this case or any other in this country, whether it concerns a mine, foundry or industrial plant.

This is why the National Miners Union fights, and why Los Mineros will continue to fight until across Mexico, every worker in this industry feels safe and protected. **Justice and social responsibility must act together, for the benefit of everyone.**

If this means they attack, defame and slander us, as they have done so maniacally and perversely over these last eight years, then we will consider ourselves **satisfied with the result of this long and endless struggle, a struggle that reveals ever more clearly the moral vacuity and nonexistent humanity of those dishonest businessmen, politicians and their respective families. In the long run, those guilty of wrongdoing will find it eating away at their conscience.**

Grupo México: Another Industrial Homicide

A new catastrophe of unforeseeable consequences is shaking Mexico, and the state of Sonora in particular; perhaps the worst in the history of this important region. Greed, corruption and the pursuit of profits at any cost, even the life and health of workers and their families, led Grupo México, directed by Germán Feliciano Larrea, to commit this latest act of industrial homicide.

A lack of control and oversight, as well as this company's criminal negligence, led the tailings dam, where the waste waters and earth from the Cananea mine are stored, to cause the spillage of 40 million litres of sulphuric acid and other dangerous and toxic chemical products used in the separation of metals, such as cyanide, cadmium, arsenic and various other minerals.

Up until now the impact of this massive incident has not been investigated or evaluated, and nor have the consequences that it will sadly bring to bear not only for fish, cattle, farmland and the ecology of the area, but also for the children, people and families who earn a living through agriculture, fishing or livestock, who are also highly dependent day-to-day on the scarce and precious water that runs through the area's rivers, irrigation channels and ponds.

As is typical with Grupo México, considered by various international organisations as undoubtedly one of the 10 least ethical companies in the entire world, they tried to keep the tragedy under wraps and made no public announcement until a few days later. This is a profound act of cowardice and criminal irresponsibility, given that many people who rely upon that water to live only found out about the disaster several days afterwards.

The consequences, then, are unimaginable, since every one of those chemicals causes cancer and is highly damaging to health. Mexico and the whole world saw photos of the dead fish and animals, in perhaps their thousands or millions, but no one has mentioned the health of the human beings that inhabit the region. This serious act of ecocide cannot go unpunished, despite Larrea, the company's shareholders and directors' attempts to hide it from public opinion, just as they did after 19th February 2006, when the Pasta de Conchos coalmine exploded, killing 65 workers in the town of San Juan de Sabinas, Coahuila, and five days later the company just turned its back, complicit with the then Secretary of Labour of the Vicente Fox administration, Francisco Javier Salazar, both accomplices of Larrea. They left 63 bodies abandoned below, which have still yet to be recovered due to the negligence, impunity and cowardice of Larrea and his associates, but also the failure of governments to force them to stand up and face the families and comply with the law.

Sonora's government has not taken serious action to investigate and use the full force of the law to punish the company, a company that wreaks destruction and death wherever it operates, whether it be here in Mexico, in Peru through the Southern Peru Copper Corporation and the possible exploitation of the Tía María mine, in Chile or the United States, where it mines in Arizona and Texas through a subsidiary company, formerly the original holding, Asarco – the American Smelting and Refining Company.

Until now, the federal government has not gotten to the bottom of this very delicate matter. Among other measures for example, the Federal Environmental Protection Agency of Mexico has apparently ruled that to prevent another tragedy of this nature, Grupo México must commit to monitoring the levels of chemical elements discharged into rivers over the next five years. If this is confirmed, it would be like putting the fox in charge of the henhouse. The other decision, which seems completely surreal and unbelievable, is to fine Grupo México a maximum of $1.38 million pesos, in contrast to the profit posted by the company over the first half of 2014 of more than 15.5 billion pesos, or barely 0.01% of their profits over the given period. This is ridiculous, a joke that will no doubt ensure Grupo México continues polluting.

As the National Miners Union, Los Mineros, has flagged on several occasions, this new industrial homicide must not go unpunished. Neither the Mexican government nor the Mexican people should remain indifferent because, based on state concessions, of all the mining groups in the country, Grupo México has its hands on the largest area of national property, sometimes with unlimited rights to exploit and abuse the contents of those lands. **This company has, therefore, become a national threat against the assets of the Mexican people. In truth, we're dealing with a parasitic group that draws on our national resources, at the expense of the savage and shameless exploitation of workers and their families.**

A decision that would be intelligent, humanitarian and in keeping with the letter of the law would be to withdraw the concession to exploit the Cananea mine from Grupo México, or at least halt its operations until the extent of this serious act of criminal negligence has been investigated by competent and independent national or foreign authorities.

The company must also be banned from repeating, as it has always done, its cowardly attempts to attack the miners union and its leaders, as a way of distracting national attention from this industrial homicide, which is what happened after the Pasta de Conchos tragedy, and as they already tried to do last week with the sensationalist scandal of the alleged Interpol red notice.

Cynicism as a Form of Government

The growth model that was introduced in Mexico a little more than three decades ago doesn't allow for changes to improve the wellbeing and quality of life for the majority of the population, let alone observe the minimum respect for their human and labour rights. Instead, economic policies that continue to be implemented, based on financial, tax, labour, energy and educational reforms, have served to reinforce the obsolete, base and immoral system of exploitation. This has generated higher inequality and a level of extreme poverty which now affects more than half of the Mexican population, people who already receive the lowest wages and income in Latin America.

A clear example of what's been going on can be found in labour policy, which has taken a real step backwards in the area of freedom of association and trade union autonomy, by breaching workers' right to freedom of association with impunity, thereby ratcheting up the inhumane exploitation of the workforce. **The upshot of this has been the authorities leaving the creation and control of trade union organisations, along with the election of their leaders, in the hands of the country's worst business owners. In other words, our republic's government has relinquished its historic duty to comply with the law and act as the guardian and protector of workers' rights.**

As we pointed out in no uncertain terms at the time, ever since Felipe Calderón and his abominable and corrupt Labour Secretary Javier Lozano Alarcón's degrading and regressive labour reform was passed, civil servants – some of whom are still to be found lodged in the current government – have acted in the interests of the business classes, because that's why they were planted there. **Their aim is to weaken or dismantle the country's democratic and independent unions.**

The PAN party governments of Vicente Fox and Felipe Calderón took a serious swing to the right in terms of labour relations, and they left behind some civil servants embedded in the current STPS to serve and obey the interests of big business, among them Deputy Secretary Secretary Rafael Avante Juárez, and the Director of the Registry of Associations, Lucio Galileo Lastra González, who have been ardently registering bogus trade unions and handing them the *toma de nota*[1]. This enables pseudo-unions to operate under the full protection of the law, **at the service of cynical and corrupt business owners who have become gangsters and bullies of the working classes, without even allowing them to express a free opinion about the organisation they would like to join.**

The latest misdemeanour on the part of these deceitful civil servants happened just last week, when they registered a new mining and metal-work trade union in favour of Coahuila's resident big-shot despot Alonso Ancira Elizondo of Grupo Acerero del Norte, so named after the shadowy privatisation of Altos Hornos de México. For over five years, Ancira has dedicated himself to intimidating, pressurising and attacking workers who have been members of the National Miners Union, Los Mineros, for 60 years or more, using hired thugs to try and force them to join his rubber-stamped circus, the so-called mining alliance, which is made up of chumps and traitors under Ancira's tyrannical boot. This is the very same man who committed major fraud over 12 years ago, spent four years in hiding in Israel and who is still in debt to the banks to the tune of around two billion dollars today, by remaining in suspension of payments.

These are the services brazenly provided by Avante, Galileo and undoubtedly some other current STPS bureaucrats. They have done so without any justification, using contracts and bogus mining trade unions, in support of the CTM, CROC and CTC among other confederations, which are mainly involved in hotel, restaurant, bar or taxi services, and never before in the metal extraction or processing industries. They're the

....

1   Taking note' (official recognition of the union's registration).

very same civil servants who gave 'plastic unions' to Grupo México's Germán Larrea and Peñoles' Alberto Bailleres under Felipe Calderón's six-year term, forcing employees to vote for these company-backed unions, sometimes using the repressive tactics of state and federal police, and even the army, but always under the threat and intimidation of job losses.

In their article published in La Jornada on July 11th, 2014, two well-known labour lawyers, the brilliant Dr. Néstor de Buen and the distinguished Óscar Alzaga, paint a clear portrait of exactly who Alonso Ancira Elizondo is, describing him as the man who presides over life and death in Coahuila state. Although he wasn't born there, he exerts unlimited power over the state, blocking the free press, manipulating local television and radio, controlling the region's chambers of commerce and trade associations and of course using hired stooges, thugs and hitmen to control trade union leaders, who are subjected to absolute suppression, domination and constant humiliation, with no principles or values. The worst of it all, as Dr. Néstor de Buen and the lawyer Alzaga have articulated, is that it shouldn't be possible to force anybody to belong to an organisation, according to the clear terms of the Universal Declaration on Human Rights.

Add to this the curious fact that **whenever these pseudo-leaders who represent the very dregs of trade unionism** celebrate their anniversary events, the Labour and Economy Secretaries send their delegates to Zacatecas, Coahuila, Sonora and other states to endorse and **praise this form of trade unionism, because it doesn't break out into strikes or struggles on the part of the workers, and instead is safely tucked into the beds and pockets of business and federal government.**

Let's see how long this shameful marriage, this cynicism, this obvious corruption –and for that matter the jobs of these public employees– will last. The true, authentic workers' movement won't let them keep up this charade, nor will it allow their irresponsibility to harden working relations in this country, **for dignity and class pride rise far above this nonsense of traitors and dishonest and complicit civil servants, who don't know anything about them, nor will they ever do.**

Labour Policy: Manipulation and Deceit

On November 21st, during the fourth activity report given by the President of the Federal Conciliation and Arbitration Committee, (JFCA by its initials in Spanish), Secretary of Labour (STPS) Minister, Alfonso Navarrete Prida, proudly declared that over the past 36 months of Enrique Peña Nieto's uninterrupted government, no strikes have broken out in the country, and that this was a highly notable achievement on the part of this administration, because they have been able to sustain a positive dialogue between capital and employment like nowhere else in the world.

Naturally, Minister Navarrete made his effusive statement, which he has already repeated on various occasions, in front of a hall full of trade union leaders of very dubious reputations and representatives from completely discredited Federa Labour Law firms. Of course the miners were not present, nor were we mentioned by name, nor me as the union's President and General Secretary, although he did make indirect reference, as he always does, to the fact that we did not agree with his statements.

And how could we, when the department and labour policy that he has headed up since this regime began have devoted themselves to simply shelving strike notices or saying that no such notices exist when strikes do actually break out. Effectively then, **this administration has consistently denied workers' right to strike, which is the very last recourse they have to defend and protect their rights against breaches or failures to comply by companies.**

Through its labour civil service, Peña Nieto's government has dedicated itself to giving complete free rein to companies to act as guardians of workers' rights, preventing them from exercising their freedom and democratic right to organise, as set out in Federal Employment Law (LFT), the Mexican Political Constitution, Convention 87 and others of the International Labour Organisation, signed and ratified by the government of Mexico some 60 years ago.

The right to strike is a universal right, whether they like it or not. In this case, however, the very labour authority itself is breaking the law and flouting its responsibilities, because of its interests in and complicity with anti-trade union business groups – groups which have no sense of social responsibility towards their staff or the communities where they operate, nor towards the environment which, left unchecked, they persist in damaging. These business owners do not act seriously and responsibly, and nor do they have any love for Mexico, as their daily acts of impunity and self-importance demonstrate.

How could we possibly celebrate Minister Navarrete's claims that there has not been a single strike in the last 36 months then, when in fact he should be ashamed of this repression of workers' free and democratic will? His claim is also entirely untrue, and to demonstrate this I will cite three cases to contradict it: only this year the workers of the National Miners Union, Los Mineros, went on strike for two weeks in August 2016 in Sections 150 and 234 of the Siderúrgica del Golfo (Gulf Iron & Steel) company based in Matamoros, Tamaulipas. These strikes were resolved in the union members' favour thanks to the tactics, unity and determination of everyone taking part, including local and national leaders. The same thing happened in March of this year in Section 271 with the miners' strike against Arcelor Mittal, based in Lázaro Cárdenas, Michoacán, which ended favourably for workers after 11 days.

Who exactly is Navarrete trying to fool, and what agreement has he made to keep national and foreign companies on his side and use false information to build their trust, when the evidence plainly contradicts him? If, as it seems, this is how every area of federal and state administration operates, they are bound to generate mistrust rather than fostering confidence, because no one, whether in or outside of Mexico, will believe them.

This government is not going to like hearing this either, but its labour and economic policies are essentially flawed, given that they do not reflect what the country really needs, nor do they demonstrate awareness of social needs. They have simply imposed a flawed model, and no one in government seeks – or is able – to analyse, understand or far less bring about change. Salaries in Mexico today are practically the lowest in all of Latin America, benefiting companies which have no sense of restraint or shame when it comes to exploiting their workforce, even going so far as to hold back consumption and demand with all the negative consequences that this has for productive activity, effectively creating greater poverty.

Even more striking though, is Navarrete's declaration that employer protection contracts do not exist in Mexico, signed and promoted behind workers' backs by some of the very trade unions that were present at that speech, as if it was their private business. This is another thing he is using intentionally to mislead people, and which allows the system of criminal exploitation of the workforce to go on and become more widespread. This demonstrates the vicious circle more clearly than ever: protection contraction, poverty wages, human and trade union rights totally denied and suppressed, while excessive profits for businessmen and politicians just keep going up.

Although they seem to think that no one realises how wrong they are on this, in fact everyone knows it. They have been criticised and complaints have even been brought before the Public Prosecution Service, the ILO, the Inter-American Commission on Human Rights and other international bodies.

Minister Navarrete Prida still made reference to me personally, indirectly as always, saying that there was one leader who always criticises this strategy. I believe it to be wrong and time will prove this, although they will no longer be in power. He dared to say that I had decided not to return to the country and that I must have my reasons, which is another of Navarrete's lies. The question is rather why they won't let me come home. He knows perfectly well why I haven't yet returned, and to feign amnesia, to put it politely, does not reflect well on him, knowing as he does as a former prosecutor that the corruption of the judicial system and buying off of politicians by some of the most dishonest businessmen in or outside of Mexico has not helped to alter or compensate for injustices. Quite the opposite: they are becoming ever more apparent, shameless and brazen.

It's not acceptable that these public servants mislead and seek to twist and play with reality and the needs of the nation, workers and Mexicans as a whole. This government turns four today, and they are running out of time to fix things, in accordance with the law, Mexico's urgent call, and its most pressing need.

The Culture of Impunity

Historically, but in particular during the last 30 years, **the decomposition of politics and business in Mexico has not only worsened the issue of corruption, but also, and this is more sensitive still, the system of complicities and influence trafficking which has become a culture of impunity.** These practices, which take place almost every day and go uninvestigated and unpunished, have caused the life of our society to significantly deteriorate, dramatically increasing inequality and reducing the prestige that Mexico held in the international community.

Not only are major conflicts and injustices not resolved, they remain forgotten and neglected, in the hope that time will bury them. This means that commonly the serious problems and abuses committed by the "powerful" in society and the friends of those in power are forgotten. The question we must ask is whether Mexico will be able to move forward under these conditions towards new stages of growth, tranquility, social peace, stability, justice and greater wellbeing.

The answer, definitively, is 'no'. As the months, years and presidential terms go by, these problems are only getting worse and becoming more deeply rooted in the life of our society. There are many, many cases, which have not been resolved according to justice and impartial legality. The examples are too many to count, but I will cite a few that infuriate us all and fill Mexicans with frustration, anger and desperation, such as the following:

The industrial homicide in the Pasta de Conchos coal mine, on the 19th of February 2006, where 65 miners lost their lives and more than ten were severely injured and suffered serious burns. Grupo México, the company truly responsible for this tragedy, and its president, Germán Larrea Mota Velasco, remain in impunity.

Alberto Bailleres' Grupo Peñoles also remains in impunity despite the terrible contamination with lead and zinc, elements that can now be detected in the blood of hundreds of children and families in Torreón, Coahuila; the mining company has caused and continues to cause irresponsible poisoning of the bodies and souls of innocent children and people who have suffered serious problems that damage their physical and mental development. This company, Peñoles, its shareholders and directors, as with Grupo México, still enjoy official protection and impunity.

What to say about the terrible tragedy of those killed and injured and hundreds of families grieving after the pitiless exploitation by Alonso Ancira Elizondo's Grupo Acero del Norte in its iron and coal mines, as well as in its steelmaking processes, with total disregard for security and hygiene in workplaces and general labour conditions? Of course this is another terrible case of ongoing impunity, worsened by the deliberate fraudulent action of Ancira and partners to keep this company in insolvency for over twelve years.

The case of children burned and killed in the ABC nursery in Hermosillo, Sonora, where those responsible for this evident and highly sensitive criminal negligence, the owners and managers, have also gone unpunished. Cases such as the shooting of over twenty young people in Tlatlaya, in the state of Mexico, without any adequate investigation to date, or anyone held responsible for these aberrant and inhumane acts.

Particularly noteworthy and infamous worldwide, is the murder and forced disappearance of the 43 student teachers in Ayotzinapa, Guerrero, which has still not been resolved, the students have not been found and there are no clear results to the investigation into this outrageous tragedy, which has left many families grieving.

I cannot fail to mention the latest industrial homicide of Germán Larrea's Grupo México, in the case of the leak of more than 400 million litres of contaminated water from the tailings dam into the Cananea and Sonora rivers, which has become the greatest tragedy in the history of mining in Mexico. Over 20 million inhabitants of the area have been affected and flora and fauna have been contaminated with highly carcinogenic substances such as cyanide, arsenic, sulphuric acid, manganese, cadmium and other chemical substances that are toxic to human health.

To date, Larrea and his accomplices have been handing out crumbs in an attempt to hush the inhabitants of various localities and regions of this area of Sonora which is important for agriculture, mining and livestock. Yet another shameful event that, to date, has ended in impunity.

The increasing handing over of national territory through mining concessions to Mexican and foreign companies, which to date and according to the reports by Roberto González Amador and the respected columnist Carlos Fernández Vega, both writing in *La Jornada*, cover almost half the country's total area. **These concessions have been granted to private companies for exploitation, despite the fact that Mexican soil and subsoil belong to the nation itself.**

In this context of the country's real situation we must ask ourselves: what are we doing as Mexican citizens, government, students, teachers, workers and leaders of civil society to slow and shift this process, which is increasingly corroding and harming our spirit and human dignity? **Either we change this system and culture of impunity or we are going to destroy ourselves as a society, as people and individuals, as human beings and we will be condemned to live in poverty, inequality, humiliation and without dignity.**

It is time to reflect, but also time to act.

Pasta de Conchos, 10 Years of Impunity

10 years ago, on 19th February 2006, one of the worse tragedies in the history of mining in Mexico took place. There was an explosion in coal mine 8 at Pasta de Conchos, in the municipality of San Juan de Sabinas, Coahuila, where 65 workers lost their lives and nine more suffered serious burns because they were not rescued or treated appropriately by the company Grupo México, owned by the insensitive businessman Germán Feliciano Larrea Mota Velasco.

At that time I called the case an industrial homicide due to the company's irresponsibility and criminal negligence in refusing to recover the bodies of the 65 mines and suspending rescue efforts after five days, not knowing if the workers were alive or dead, causing deep suffering to their families. With this inhumane decision, bearing in mind that even in warfare the fallen are not left on the battlefield, Grupo México and Larrea aimed to spinelessly avoid having over 65 lawsuits brought against them because in their arrogance they never improved the unsafe conditions that were the norm in the mine and were repeatedly cited by members of the Mixed Commission for Security and Hygiene. The National Miners Union, Los Mineros, constantly demanded their immediate improvement, but with their miserable and high-handed attitude of the company's board of directors, headed by Germán Larrea and Xavier García de Quevedo, refused to take action.

2006 was the last year of government under Vicente Fox and his wife Marta Sahagún, both with interests and complicities clearly exhibited and recognised with Larrea and his company through, among other cases, Fundación Vamos México, created especially to obtain large

127

donations from Larrea and other businessmen who would contribute to fattening the future ex-president and his leading lady wife's retirement fund. Of course, thanks to **these donations and contributions** Germán Larrea, Alberto Bailleres González, Alonso Ancira Elizondo, Jilio Villarreal Guajardo and **many others received the protection and cover-ups they required to commit all manner of abuses and violations of the rule of law, without being denounced or charged**, show by the fact that from then on they have been in a situation of total, lacerating impunity vis-à-vis the whole of society and not just workers.

With the coming of Vicente Fox's PAN to power and the election of Felipe Calderón to the Presidency, as he himself said, whatever it was that went on, insecurity, corruption and influence trafficking accelerated enormously. The contributions of the aforementioned businessmen, which were used to finance political campaigns or the shady dealings and personal funds were compensated with mining, gas, electricity, petroleum, tourist development and other concessions, with PAN governors accepting the imposition of public functionaries specifically chosen to safeguard and increase the business interests of those same contributors.

And so we suffered under various Secretaries of State in PAN governments and members of the Legislative and Judicial powers who were designated or imposed and came from that group of opportunists, mercenaries and influence traffickers pursuing personal business interests without scruples, moral quality or professional ethics. To mention some who where seriously responsible for the shocking tragedy at Pasta de Conchos, we have Francisco Javier Salazar, ex-Secretary for Labour under Fox, who was an active supplier of chemical products for Larrea and Grupo México in his personal businesses located in San Luis Potosí. His son-in-law was the delegate for the Secretary for Labour in Coahuila when the explosion took place and 65 Mexican miners were tragically killed, 63 of whose bodies remain abandoned inside the sealed mine, only 120 metres down. Moreover, Salazar's son was named by Fox as the first president of the Nation Energy Regulating Commission, which is the body that awards concessions for the exploitation of gas, with Grupo México being the principal beneficiary and recipient of the first concession in 2006, the same year as the tragedy.

Calderón later named the detestable Javier Lozano Alarcón as the next Secretary for Labour to further cover for Larrea and Grupo México. **Lozano is in the running against Salazar for the dishonourable title of having been the worst Secretaries of that department in Mexico's history.** It is said in political circles that he was on the payroll of Grupo México and was, is and will be in charge of protecting Larrea and his ex-boss Felipe Calderón's criminal irresponsibility. He was also campaign coordinator for Calderón and collected funds such as those 205 million dollars from China's Zhenli Yegón which disappeared without a trace. In the 2012 federal elections, Lozano was installed as Senator of Puebla to cover Felipe Calderón's back and his own.

The other case of public disgrace was the designation of Fernando Gómez Mont, Larrea's criminal lawyer, who is still in that role and came to be named Interior Secretary, or as is said in the political world, the virtual vice-presidency of Mexico. **Gómez Mont did and continues to do everything from the same trench to cover for Larrea and attack all those who oppose or represent a challenge to his interests. His abjection and servility degrade and sully the legal profession and the correct application of justice which is so lacking in Mexico.** In the same situation are the ex-attorneys of the Republic Eduardo Medina Mora, Daniel Cabeza de Vaca, Jesús Murillo Karam; the current sub-Secretary for Labour Rafael Avante and others besides.

Today, 10 years later, thanks to these immoral and perverse individuals, the bodies of 63 mine workers have still not been recovered because no effort was every made to rescue them, unlike in the case of 33 miners in Chile, which became a moral, human and political victory for workers, unions, families, the company and the conservative government of Sebastián Piñera in that great Latin American country. In Mexico there has never been a professional independent investigation into the tragedy and its causes, and much less any attempt to punish those responsible with the full force of the law. There has equally been no meaningful compensation for the widows and families in terms of justice and dignity, which constitutes a huge social debt for Grupo México and those governing the Republic that remains unpaid.

The question to be asked of the current government is how long will it take to act on the demand for recovery, the fair compensation of families and the punishment of those responsible. **How many more human tragedies have to happen for there to be justice and an end to impunity?** It would be incredible if the Mexican government led by Enrique Peña Nieto could provide a definitive solution to this unjust situation.

And this, in the context of the visit to Mexico by the great Pope Francis, who has made clear proposals, not just for peace and reconciliation, but also for justice, respect and dignity towards those who have less and have been abandoned. The image of Mexico would grow enormously if they were to follow and **honour the Pope's call for human betterment. It is time for an end to impunity.**

Miners Continue to Demand Truth and Justice

10 years have passed since the terrible tragedy at the Pasta de Conchos coal mine, in the municipality of San Juan de Sabinas, Coahuila, caused by German Feliciano Larrea Mota Velasco's Grupo México, and we are still in the dark about what really happened. There has never been an appropriate independent investigation to determine the causes of the explosion and to punish those responsible for the industrial homicide, which plunged the families of the 65 miners who died into mourning, with the full weight of the law. Justice has still not been done and this is the third government which has pretended to make decisions that are quickly forgotten or abandoned.

Hardly anyone is interested in uncovering the truth. Over the course of this decade all those involved – businessmen, politicians and enemies of trade union organisations – have covered up for each other, all with the same attitude of cowards, traitors and charlatans who have thrived and continue to thrive on the misfortune and human sacrifice of decent and responsible workers. But there is a similar lack of concern from those who could bring justice and punish the criminal negligence of shareholders, directors and accomplices in the exploitation and plundering of the country's natural resources at any cost, including workers' lives and health.

And even today they continue with finances or manipulated publications which attempt to divert attention and avoid direct responsibility for this industrial and social crime. In doing so they use all kinds of tricks,

131

media and distorted information with those who seek to hide the truth and cover up their responsibility for the terrible tragedy that changed the lives of 65 Mexican families.

The latest action is to use even the magazine *Proceso* to publish a totally unfounded report to distort reality, including an alleged agreement that seeks to exonerate Grupo México and its directors and members of the board and the labour authorities. What a shame and what a disgrace that they still resort to such evil actions and that certain media accept them, instead of courageously and objectively showing the truth. In the face of all this vindictiveness and slander, we in the National Mineworkers Union have for 10 years repeatedly explained the truth of the mining conflict and demonstrated that nothing can stop us on the road to demanding truth and justice, despite the malicious reports and ongoing dirty campaign against the miners.

During the government of Carlos Salinas de Gortari and amid intense privatization policy, which ended with State intervention and regulation in the economy by way of parastatal companies, contractors' agreements were invented on the pretext of giving those companies competitiveness and flexibility. What's more, outsourcing or third-party companies created a new form of workforce known as contracting in addition to the existing form, that of permanent and temporary unionised workers. Since then, pressure from governments over the last 30 years has forced many unions to yield to these trends and reduce corporate responsibility towards their members.

Labour policy then became a fully business-oriented policy with the strengthening of monopolies, the emergence of many new fortunes created under privatization, misappropriation and lack of social and political commitment to the interests of the nation and of Mexicans. What the new investors who acquired State companies and consortia actually wanted to do and are still trying to bring about is to get rid of the unions, particularly democratic unions, and the collective labour contracts which burden them with responsibilities they would rather remove, destroy or control with any form of institutional support and governmental complicity. Unfortunately in many cases they have succeeded.

Collective bargaining or temporary agreements can never exonerate or relieve companies of their essential responsibility not only for production, but to protect and care for the lives and health of all workers. What neither Germán Larrea or Xavier Garcia de Quevedo, president of Industrial Minera México, responsible for the operation of Pasta de Conchos, or any other engineer, administrator or manager can avoid, is their responsibility in the industrial homicide that took the lives of 65 Mexican miners, the result of ambition, greed and criminal negligence.

In many countries, and Mexico is no exception, most journalists and media covering labour issues come from the middle or upper class. The same is true of the politicians responsible for implementing labor policy and supposedly defending of the rights of the working class. This means that little is published on the actions and life of unions apart from sensationalist reports or frequent attacks on organizations and leaders in order to discredit, weaken and divide them and seek their submission or permanent destruction.

Of course, some union leaders succumb and prefer not to fight for their members or to defend their honour and dignity. But that not only creates and fosters the impunity and corruption of businessmen, politicians and the leaders themselves, given that in most cases all feel untouchable, sharing among themselves the wealth generated by complicity and immorality, and the deepening inequality in Mexico. It also shuts down opportunities for the democracy and transparency required for healthy, fair and balanced social, economic and political activity.

It's Time for New Politics

The New Labour Philosophy

Neoliberal culture has, rather unsuccessfully so far, attempted to prevent workers organising themselves into unions and different associations. Faced with this failure, neoliberals have opted to obstruct, corrupt, confuse and divide, sullying the image of true and authentic social and union leaders.

Unfortunately, the ambition of certain individuals and their lack of principles and values, as well as the power of money, have meant that they have willingly become puppets of the dominant classes, going as far as whole-heartedly joining that group of corrupters, traitors, sell-outs and the civil servants who are complicit in this perverse and immoral strategy. But this behaviour has done no more than generate one of the degrading deviations of union, business and government life. The workers' true fight for unity, loyalty and class solidarity is far above wickedness and unchecked complicity.

The future of trade unionism is not at stake because the general and natural tendency of labour relations is and will always be to freely organise to defend and protect labour and human rights. This happens from a perspective of solidarity and common strength so that production systems develop calmly, efficiently and fairly.

The current government, together with ambitious and insatiably greedy businesspeople, have failed to realise that the world is overtaking them and they are being exposed as the true guilty parties of an economic and social failure that will have its repercussions in the immediate development of our society. This serious error has caused a lack of security, self-confidence sensitivity, vision and preparation on the part of the country's political leaders and of many businessmen who have not allowed workers to participate more in planning and productive decision-making.

The next government will have the huge task of getting Mexico back on track and changing its economic policy, now cold and dehumanised, for one that really listens, corrects and resolves the needs and injustices that Mexicans endure. They must also make the nation's activity more balanced and reasonable.

The traditional production model in Mexico has reached its limit. The economy cannot continue to grow based on systems that privilege the unchecked concentration of wealth in a few hands and the abusive exploitation of the workforce. **However, the country can no longer wait tolerantly while the ignorance and arrogance of a few people destroy the hopes of the great majority who desire a profound change.**

The design of a new strategy has to be thorough – as it has been in countries like China, Brazil, Japan, Argentina and others – and new production relations will have to be based on much clearer concepts of social responsibility and shared responsibility between businesspeople and workers. This must cover the whole range of our society's productive powers to allow alternatives and new participatory models to be incorporated.

Mexico needs, and is going to need a new labour philosophy, supported by respect and dignity, and the participation of workers in processes, plans and programmes, as well as in the strategies for a new system of shared growth. **The country needs to adopt a model in which all businesspeople see workers as partners and not as simple objects of exploitation or operational instruments.** In making decisions and preparing initiatives they must have and develop greater knowledge and experience, with which they will be able to contribute to balanced production growth and increased justice.

The benefits obtained from this new labour philosophy will become social profits, which could be reinvested to create more jobs, sources and centres for work, as well as greater efficiency and productivity and a fairer development of economic activity.

In Mexico, although there has been a lot of talk about applying a culture of work we have moved towards one that more tightly controls salaries and halts the purchasing power of those salaries, and as a result stops the economic demand of workers in the market. The opposite should be the case: we need a model that stimulates the market with better remuneration and participation, linked to specific strategies of productivity, so as to improve and strengthen the purchasing power of wage-earners, consumption capacity, economic demand and the general wellbeing of the population.

From another perspective, **what we need is a new culture among employers** whereby they understand and respect workers, a culture that brings together social responsibility and does not obtain concession or benefits from society solely in order to achieve the objective of maximum profit. We must have guarantees that justice, dignity and the true search for the greatest possible happiness for workers will prevail, so that all may benefit.

This is what I have been suggesting as the essence of the new trade unionism for the 21st century, which asserts a new labour philosophy and a new economic policy.

The Last Chance

Recent decades have brought losses for Mexico in development, national dignity and social justice. These losses have touched by the whole nation, its people and Mexico's modern history. I would like to paint a positive picture, but no other conclusion can be reached given the circumstances, not even with the most optimistic of attitudes.

It is enough to look at the number of Mexicans living in poverty: over 50 million. And the number of the rich and very rich, who barely exceed 300 families, and among them, the 30 supposed 'owners' of Mexico. Or the numbers of dead and disappeared in the absurd war on drug trafficking, who between them amount to over 150,000 people. Or the rates of unemployment, with over 14 million job losses across formal and informal employment. Or levels of corruption, both inside and outside government, that are difficult to calculate but reach hundreds of billions of pesos. Or equally, the real loss of the rule of law in fundamental areas such as the impunity under which all sorts of crimes are committed, both common law and white collar crimes executed by well-off people who break the law and are even congratulated for doing so.

Or the figures for Mexican migrants to the United States who go in search of the work they are unable to find here, who number more than **30 million people** according to dramatic real-life studies, which include both previous migrants and those who are leaving today, **who together constitute a new migrant country**. This is on top of the losses of opportunities to positive human development, which can equally be measured in millions. It's a truly bleak panorama.

The last decade in particular has been harmful for Mexico and for Mexicans. No one with even the slightest awareness of social reality can suggest that these last 12 years have brought progress and economic and social development. On the contrary, all the evidence and real-life hard facts show us that we face a serious national disaster under the conservative governments led by the National Action Party. What Vicente Fox's government did and what Felipe Calderón's continues to do is to devalue the public sector and seriously damage the country's image abroad, bombarding the population with dishonest fantasies about the real state of the economy, with the complicity of the most powerful media outlets that are duly aligned with what they falsely call a national project. They infuse all their messages with the fear of change, an irrational fear of things being better, but true transformation can only be achieved by ceasing to reject new options for progress, and by fighting for a fairer model of economic and social policy.

The best way that we Mexicans can move forward, if we are to change the way things are, is simply via legal means and especially by way of elections, bravely standing together to rebuild our country instead of being scared of change. In 10 days we will cast our votes. Contrary to what some surveys have exaggeratedly claimed, this election is not yet decided. It was not decided beforehand when the possible presidential candidates started campaigning, nor is today, faced with the evidence of new public demonstrations which have been recorded among voters, in large part in response to this new media campaign which would have us believe that the 1ˢᵗ July election has already been won by a wide margin.

But in this strategy of injecting insecurity and uncertainty into society, such adjustments to electoral preferences are not registered by the media who prefer nothing to change in our country and want everything to carry on like it is today. **They no longer even play at *Gatopardo*, that is the practice of always making small changes so that everything remains the same**, instead they invent and broadcast, veiled by very dubious surveys, when the massive popular vote has not yet taken place.

This is our last chance. The last one we have to replace a mistaken vision that would hold us on a path to ruin. Either Mexico regenerates itself or we are in for an even darker, more destructive and bleaker period than that of recent lost decades. In these elections, like in none ever before, the country's future is truly at stake. Either we fearlessly decide our own destiny and choose the path of profound change in the country's political, economic and social structures, or the interests of a few will hold the huge majority in a state of fear. This is essentially what is at stake in the national debate and at polling stations.

Faced with this outlook, all that remains to be said is that enough is enough of Mexicans being manipulated. We were previously manipulated through the buying, coercion and co-opting of votes. Today it is through the manipulative use of television and other media, which answer to the interests of those individuals who want Mexico to carry on with its ruthless exploitation of human labour, low salaries, growing unemployment, insecurity and the impunity of the powerful people and their criminal acts. Mexico must change. It is unacceptable that we should elect the bad guys because they are familiar and the good guys are forgotten because they spring from the conscience of a people who have taken on massive challenges in the past and have overcome them, always with new hopes for a better future.

We must lose the contemptible fear of change. Over 2,000 years ago, the Roman poet Horace said: "He who lives in fear will never be free". Today, we Mexicans are facing our last opportunity. Either we change the path to disaster we are on, or we will destroy our great country even more.

One Day Longer

In memory of Lynn Williams and Napoleón Gómez Sada

A few days ago, on June 21st, a sensitive and remarkable tribute was paid to Lynn Russell Williams in Toronto, Ontario Canada, the first Canadian International President of the United Steelworkers union, the USW, marking a profound shift in the North American attitude and trade union struggle towards greater democracy and social justice.

Lynn died on May 5th in Toronto at the age of 89 years old. He led the union for 11 years, from 1983 to 1994, and was re-elected three times during that time. Through Leo Gerard and Ken Neumann, I regularly met and dealt with Lynn over my recent years of exile in Canada. He was a great friend, an admirable person, an extraordinary leader and an inspiration to the working class, who reminded me a lot of Napoleón Gómez Sada. Both men lived through tough times for the industry and employment as a result of a series of economic recessions that posed a real threat to workers, trade unions and leaders as eminent as Lynn or Gómez Sada. One such challenge faced by Gómez Sada in 1986 was the bankruptcy and closure of what was then the leading metalwork company in Mexico, the Monterrey Iron and Steel Foundry.

Lynn represented the best of the workers movement and was always a truly brave an intelligent social activist. **Like Gómez Sada, he believed in dignity and equality, and was committed to continually improving the lives of workers and their families**, as well as pushing for better working conditions. He joined the Steelworkers at the end of the 1940s, while

145

working for the John Inglis Company in Toronto. He rose up through the ranks until he was made Director of USW District 6; he later became International Secretary and finally, its President.

One of Lynn's great achievements as leader was to maintain the strength and power of one of the most progressive and democratic trade unions in North America and the world today. During the 1980s, certain people were already getting USW's obituary ready and predicting its downfall. At the time, the iron and steel industry had begun to suffer serious problems that manifested themselves in closures, liquidations and massive staff lay-offs at a number of metal and steel works. Some commentators were speculating about the demise of this incredible organisation.

The early years of this difficult and complex period went by, and United Steelworkers was soon shaken by the sudden death of their then International President Lloyd McBride in 1983. As USW's International Secretary, Lynn Williams was elected as leader, and took on the daunting task of surmounting the enormous challenges and cyclical events that were doing so much damage to his proud union.

Like Napoleón Gómez Sada, who would have celebrated his 100th birthday this year, Lynn managed to overcome this period of global crisis and turmoil in the iron and steel industries, thanks to his immense leadership skills and his unprecedented ability to innovate. Both men played a crucial role in developing new techniques and strategies for collective bargaining with businesses and many politicians that were truly novel, and they made decisions and devised ways of radically restructuring the entire steel manufacturing industry.

Integrity, and the visionary idealism to achieve greater equality in social struggles were the outstanding principles and qualities shared by both leaders. Another key attribute was their pragmatism, which allowed them to demand greater respect and social responsibility from companies as they worked towards achieving justice. They were men who worked hard for and protected families. Their intelligence and instincts gave them a leadership style that showed the working classes and their allies the way forward.

Leo Gerard, the current International President of the USW union puts it clearly: "Lynn Williams kept the union together through the worst of times. He demonstrated that he was a leader of great generosity and ingenuity, securing deals and agreements that saved as much as possible for industry, while still protecting salaries and benefits for workers."

Lynn, like Gómez Sada, proved time and time again that he had the strength, the standing and the intelligence required to take on company directors and corporate shareholders, as well as the most conservative politicians in the system. **Nonetheless, the thing that gave them both the most satisfaction was working actively alongside their union members and enjoying the warmth, loyalty and backing of the workers whom they felt profoundly privileged to serve and support.**

Lynn Williams' book of memoirs, which was published in 2011 in collaboration with Toronto University in Canada and Cornell University in the United States, is called *One Day Longer*. He regularly used to attend picket lines and lock-outs when strikes broke out, to give encouragement to his colleagues involved in disputes. When moments of weariness and despondency arose, he would ask them: how much longer are we going to go on resisting? And together they would all answer: "one day longer" than the companies. They were the sort of leaders that are so desperately needed in today's trade unions, marking themselves out as wise visionaries and sensitive human beings, always ready to help others.

Solidarity, forever.

A New Trade Unionism for the 21ˢᵗ Century

In view of the unpaid social debts that Mexico is confronting, both the population and government must reflect on the matter maturely and seriously, because if these problems are not tackled wholeheartedly, in a calm and constructive spirit, they might lead us to unwanted crisis situations that would be deeper than those we are already experiencing. **One of these crucial issues is the trade unionism of our time**, which covers and influences the labour relations of all Mexicans, whether or not they are affiliated to workers' organisations, and has direct repercussions for the possibilities of real true economic and social development that benefits the great majority of people. On more occasions than is desirable, the issue is approached without a real knowledge of its nature and profound importance.

Those of us who have had the experience of working in the union world have a clear conscience that unionism is, above all, an absolute necessity, and no country can move forwards peacefully and calmly in terms of labour without it. The conservative or reactionary regimes that in Mexico and across the world have attempted to get rid of unions have failed throughout history. Governments that have tried to restrict or destroy union freedom, splitting up unions, pursuing and assassinating their leaders, trying to submit workers to interests that are not their own, have failed and will continue to do so. They are likely to keep on trying, not without first seriously wounding workers and their families.

The lessons of recent years have demonstrated that we unionists form part of a process that is constantly changing and transforming, unfortunately not always for the better. Throughout this continuous process of adaptation to change we must be conscious of consolidating advances and achievements that have been obtained throughout the union struggle and prepare ourselves to face up with dignity, strength and efficiency to the challenges that we will meet. In these conditions, it is inadmissible that they attempt to wipe out with one blow the entirety of the experience that has been accumulated by the unions' constant struggle to improve conditions of wellbeing for workers and their communities. The unions are alive and will continue to exist, despite the mistaken ideas of those people who were or have been dogmatically malformed. **Since the introduction of salaried work in the modern world, there have been organisations that through unity and solidarity defend and protect the interests and rights of their members.**

Just as certain countries have undergone labour reforms that have only resulted in greater inequality and aggravated social problems, as is the case in Greece, Spain, Italy and Ireland, there are also nations that without having adopted great changes in their labour legislation have achieved greater efficiency in the application of an economic policy that promotes development and increases opportunities to gain dignified and well-paid jobs that generate a higher quality of life. As a result they have become flexible, productive and efficient countries with the world's lowest levels of corruption and inequality, stemming from the highest level of unionisation – over 85 percent of the workforce – as is the situation in the Scandinavian countries: Sweden, Norway, Finland and Denmark.

I do not share the view that we Mexicans are conformists, as proved by the countless expressions of struggle and resistance against the ruthless injustice and exploitation of labour. The harder and more violent the repression of the working class, the more energetic the popular response has been. Examples within our country date back to the 19th century, such as the mutualist and professional unions that later became the unions of the 20th century and struggled hard for their existence, confronting repression like that exacted by Porfirio Díaz's dictatorial regime, which led to the massacres in Cananea, Sonora, and Río Blanco, Veracruz in 1906 and 1907.

We have had a whole century of union evolution and transformation since the 1917 Constitution and the regimes that were born from that.

There is no doubt that historic experience supplies us with sufficient good judgement to visualise new directions for unionism. Although the unions, due to their initial weakness, had to work in strict alliance with the governments that came out of the 1917 Revolution, it is now time for us to revise this alliance. **Today international union alliances and solidarity allow us to clearly distinguish between progressive governments and those that are in the service of employers and business owners as part of a global model of exploitation of the workforce and natural resources.** This has been the case in Mexico from 1982 until the present day, when the old powers of social privilege have formed partnerships to once more impose their selfish interests above those of society.

In Mexico we need a new unionism that responds to the constant changes and the needs of workers and organisations in the 21st century. Only by strengthening the positives and with a process of constant improvement will Mexico be able to progress towards a society founded on justice and equality. But this must not be achieved by allowing others to trample the achievements that unionists and their allies have made over a century of existence and struggle, such as the fundamental guarantees of workers, which since the first of June 2010 are considered as human rights, including freedom of association, autonomy, collective contracting and striking, which the current enemies of the working class are trying to destroy.

At the moment the Senate has the serious responsibility of either acting in line with this, or simply submitting to the dictates of the employers' class and the National Action Party. Senators must, from a legal and ethical point of view, avoid moving backwards in history; instead they must move us forwards towards a nation with greater justice and dignity. This is a historic opportunity to correct the conservative tendencies and postures that mean to drive towards a new type of slavery which would be formalised by the initial labour reform project.

Vision and Change from Vancouver

Once again, the spirit of vision and change was expressed during an excellent meeting in Vancouver, concerning analysis and discussion about the current situation in Mexico, the prospects for the mining, metal and steelwork industry, and its future national growth. It was felt that if productivity is to increase at every level, it must be built on coordinated efforts, effective operations and clear will between production factors.

It is incredible that after more than seven years of aggression and political persecution against the National Miners Union, Los Mineros, and its leaders, the organisation remains solid, united, growing, changing and with prospects for development and welfare that would greatly help Mexico to streamline and civilise economic activity and to open up new and improved opportunities for all through this noteworthy example.

At the Vancouver meeting between distinguished leaders of more than 40 companies of this crucial national industry sector and the leaders of Los Mineros, the National Miners Union, it was reiterated once more for all those who had not wanted to listen, contribute ideas and even take part, that they will remain forever marginalised in the annals of history for their regressive and conservative mentalities, which looked for Mexico and its workers to return to 18th and 19th century levels of exploitation and injustice, a sort of slavery in disguise.

Those four companies such as Grupo México, Grupo Peñoles, Grupo Acerero del Norte and Villacero that currently live and grow on an outmoded foundation of abuse, subjugation and greed, will end up on society's rubbish tip, their image totally ruined and debased by reckless and

153

blind ambition, which will be the measure of their own downfall and ruin as despicable inhabitants of this earth.

On the other hand, the large national and foreign companies that voluntarily attended this event were recognised and honoured for having contributed to the process of ongoing change and to the nation's industrial development, based on equality, productivity, collaboration and mutual respect. Some of these companies deserve to be mentioned, such as DeAcero, Compañía Occidental Mexicana, Fertinal, Arcelor Mittal –the largest private producer of steel in the world–, Gold Corp, Bombardier Transportation, Endeavour Silver, First Majestic, Primero Compañía Minera and many more. The proposals and agreements emerging from this meeting, held at the Miners' Union's initiative, are an example of –and an integral step towards– establishing a new model of shared prosperity that benefits both workers and companies alike, as well as the industry and country in general.

Those four companies that use irrational and reckless exploitation and injustice, with limitless arrogance and self-importance, are the same companies that threatened and blackmailed the country with leaving and taking their investments elsewhere if the new taxes on mining were applied to them. The new fiscal measures have already been approved and they still haven't left, and nor are they going to do so. **The back-peddling of these companies is explained by two fundamental things:** 1) They can't leave with the earth, nor the minerals contained in its subsoil, that belong to the Mexicans, to the nation, and which they exploit on the basis of a concession, with no regard for the future of Mexico. 2) They are not going to find any better place to invest that would give them such profits, privileges and influence over political power, which they have been abusing for the past twenty years at least, since as far back as the *Salinista*[1] privatisations.

So Mexicans, at ease, because the richest aren't about to leave us. Their extortion and intimidation is a way of impressing inexpert,

....

1   Adjective from Carlos Salinas de Gortari, neoliberal reformist PRI party politician who was President of Mexico from 1988 to 1994.

pompous or crony politicians with no political strength. The Mexican public is resisting, and has resisted such attacks, blackmail and threats at other times in history, where similar individuals have evidently failed. Mexico is greater, much greater than these characters who have made an indecent living on the backs of the workers and Mexicans that they look down upon.

Their back peddling goes hand-in-hand with their barefacedness and cynicism, along with that of their collaborators and accomplices from the offices of mercenary lawyers at their service and the unscrupulous types that oversee the media or write in the press, motivated merely by obsequiousness and corruption. These include Pedro Ferriz de Con, Darío Celis, Alberto Barranco Chavarría and many others besides who denigrate the journalistic profession, their conduct, sarcastic jibes and writing style a reflection of their non-existent moral quality. Today, but even more so tomorrow, they will find themselves dead and buried in the most ignominious obscurity.

Benito Juárez said that there are unqualified lawyers and unlawyered qualifications. The same thing happens with the shameful false journalism, which is simply used irresponsibly to serve the dark interests that blackmail Mexico and attack the highest level politicians alike.

Workers and Development

This week, from the 16th to the 18th April, in Vancouver, Canada, the National Policy Conference organised by United Steelworkers (USW) is taking place. On 52 occasions this exceptional meeting has brought people together to analyse and discuss important issues such as global strategic alliances, business and the economy, the challenges of corporate power, the comprehensive review of what we have learnt from the past and what the future will bring for a new generation of unionists and politicians.

We were invited to make official speeches along with a considerable number of leaders, including Leo W. Gerard, international president of USW; Ken Neumann and Steve Hunt, national directors for Canada and district 3 of USW respectively, and hosts of this meeting; Jyrki Raina, secretary general of the world's biggest union, IndustriALL Global Union with 50 million members; Thomas Mulcair, leader of the New Democratic Party and leader of the opposition in Canada; myself as president and secretary general of the Mexican mining workers, metalworkers and steelworkers, and other political and union leaders from the United States, the United Kingdom, Australia, South Africa, Peru, and from across five continents.

The messages and opinions that we have heard have lead us to reflect deeply on the future of society, the working class, inequality and injustice, the risks implicit in social peace such as excessive ambition and greed, the lack of awareness of the impact on coming generations, ignorance, irresponsibility and unchecked exploitation. Of course it would have been impossible to leave specific issues of jobs, security, the environment, health, and working conditions out of the passionate discussions, and they were tackled with great intelligence. No room was left for doubt about how we can be better prepared to face up to the challenges of brutal capitalism, to improve labour harmony and tranquillity, as well as how to project a new and fresher image of the world union movement.

This conference will draw to a close today. It has been a real success for the almost one thousand delegates, and it will have to grow and expand and cast its message wide **because these forums must provide the best solutions for reducing marginalisation and deprivation, and strategies that will allow faster progress in the construction of a better world in which there is more respect, justice and equality**. These qualities generate greater stability, peace and progress for everyone, not just for a few.

In Mexico we will have to review and assimilate the conclusions that will allow us to change the direction of politics more profoundly and efficiently, and thus move towards a new stage of development, building on the foundation of our membership of the North American Free Trade Agreement (NAFTA) together with Canada and the United States. All of us, workers, government, businesspeople and society in general, must take note of the conclusions of this meeting, which are framed by demands for equality and fairness, because none of the three countries, although they have very different levels of development, can pretend to have resolved the deep social inequalities that exist within their borders. That is why we have proposed that the Free Trade Agreement to which we have signed up should become a real plan for cooperation and development between the three countries.

This is the only way it will be possible to turn the international cooperation that is implicit in the NAFTA, but which today remains incomplete, into a solid tool for the economic and social development of the three nations. We cannot and must not ignore the fact that the United States and Canada are facing difficult social challenges, despite a lopsided and biased message that in those counties there is no poverty or destitution, because there is. In the particular case of Mexico it is important to develop this new vision of international cooperation through which, while maintaining respect for the sovereignty of each nation, we will be able to channel the resources and efforts that are currently concentrated solely on commercial activity therefore do not press the buttons of real economic progress, namely equal opportunities and respect for the rights and interests of all sectors of each one of the countries involved.

The first step to take in this direction must be in the area of labour cooperation between the three countries, because here agreement on the issue between the signatory governments has been practically dead letter. Workers in Canada, the United States and Mexico, facilitated by miners, have contributed a wealth of ideas about how to turn the labour cooperation agreement into a genuine commitment to social development. This should, by all means, serve the interests of employers, but it must also have a substantial parallel focus on how to resolve issues of well-paid work, fair settlement of labour disputes and respect for the freedom and autonomy of union organisations. Such an initiative will eliminate the increasing employment instability and inhuman forms of exploitation that are proper to the brutal capitalism practiced in all our nations, but which is thrown into clearer relief in Mexico than in the other two.

Mexico's new government has the opportunity to enter into this new vision of international development efforts. The two previous National Action Party governments were deaf and blind to the demands of genuine economic and social development in Mexico, and they completely turned their backs on the possibilities offered by international cooperation for development.

Long Live IndustriALL Global Union

"The struggle continues" is the slogan this important organization chose to celebrate its second world congress in the city of Rio de Janeiro, Brazil, held from Monday 3rd to Friday 7th October this year. IndustriALL is the world's largest group of workers from free and democratic trade unions, with over 50 million members from 140 countries, to which the miners of Mexico are affiliated, and in me they have the only leader on the international executive committee representing workers from across our country, as well Central America and the Caribbean.

This great global union was born in 2012, when the first founding congress was held in Copenhagen, Denmark. It was the result of the integration and merger of three federations which had existed for many years: IMF, the International Metalworkers' Federation; ICEM, the International Federation of Chemical, Energy, Mine and General Workers' Unions, as well as ITGLWF, the International Textile, Garment and Leather Workers' Federation.

IndustriALL represents the workforce in many industries, from extraction (mining, oil and gas), processing (steel, automotive, aerospace, mechanical equipment) as well as services and food, footwear and clothing, among others. One of the key objectives which defines the commitment and strength of this powerful organisation lies in its great conviction that **all workers of the world are entitled to fair remuneration for the fruits of their labour.** It seeks, among its goals, to create a global community through which to share power and opportunities. **Its fundamental demand is for respect for the human rights of all and the right to live**

in dignity, security, peace and solidarity, without prejudice and injustice.

The meeting in Rio de Janeiro to develop the work of the second IndustriALL world congress aimed to adopt a political resolution as a support and extension of the **2016-2020 action plan, which sets out the objectives and goals of this great organisation.** Given the constant attacks on the right to freedom of association by big business and governments, its key priorities are to increase organizational programmes and union membership, and to strengthen collective bargaining.

On the issue of inequality, IndustriALL clearly identified through their research that one percent of the world's richest people now own more wealth than the remaining 99 per cent. This global inequality is a real and potential social and economic crisis, because the differences between countries and internally also between classes grow every day.

From this analysis it is patently clear that workers are constantly losing in terms of their real incomes, as well as their working conditions and social protection. The groups which are currently most disadvantaged are those most affected by the inequality that is increasing day by day. This is why some global organizations such as the OECD (Organisation for Economic Co-operation and Development) and the ILO (International Labour Organisation) in their reports entitled 'In It Together: Why Less Inequality Benefits All' and 'World Employment and Social Outlook: Trends 2015', respectively, are calling on governments to adopt effective measures to combat growing inequalities.

Wage inequality has increased since 2000, a trend that has been exacerbated by the expansion of job insecurity. Poverty rates are increasingly high among temporary workers and freelancers who are not members of or affiliated to any union. **This complex and awful situation of inequality prevents economic growth and increases exploitation and poverty.**

Moreover, IndustriALL says that impunity in the supply chain of a profoundly unfair and unsustainable model prevails in industrial sectors. Multinational companies extend their production to domestic suppliers and assembly plants that usually do not guarantee a living wage, union rights or secure jobs and places of work. This system generates a global race to the bottom which further deteriorates working conditions, as the governments that accept them compete to attract investment at the expense of the welfare of workers and society as a whole. For example, through tax exemptions or extraction of raw materials without leaving added value in the provider country.

Corporate social responsibility does not exist, or has not been able to pick up on violations and abuses of rights, because it is a tool at the service of companies rather than workers. This instrument has also failed to significantly improve wages or working hours, or guarantee universal respect for the right of workers to freely join the union of their choice. And for that they use to their advantage the political and economic relations of complicity with federal and state governments, boards of conciliation and arbitration and unions that have many ghosts employer protection contracts.

Faced with this situation, IndustriALL still has a long way to go to build power and social justice in the world. **The unification and solidarity to achieve dignity are a great challenge.**

Shared Prosperity: A Proposal

Today's world faces significant challenges as opportunities become increasingly difficult and complex to grasp. The results of the economic crises in Europe, the United States and every continent mean all community organizations need to be united, alert and to work in solidarity.

Democracy and freedom are under constant threat and attack from the most conservative powers, and not only in Mexico, Latin America, Asia or Africa, but also in Europe and the United States. Liberalism has conquered the world, becoming the key driver of inequality by concentrating wealth in fewer and fewer hands. The doctrine of serving the interests of the most privileged and powerful – and in particular large corporations, banking groups and bankers – ahead of the needs of the working classes and the general public has been the political orthodoxy on both sides of the Atlantic for some time now. **Generations to come are condemned to face lower standards of living, greater suffering and poorer outcomes in terms of well-being.**

The unemployed and their families bear the greatest burden of the economic crises, but the effects are also felt by a wider section of society. Inequality remains a clear and potentially growing danger, jeopardizing social harmony and job security.

Today we should pause to reflect on where we are going, and what lies ahead for Mexico and the rest of the world. Paul Streeten, a distinguished professor from Oxford University, England, who supervised my thesis, said that we must all intellectualize our ideas, step back and reflect on the problems, challenges and alternatives we face, alongside taking a more active role in analyzing, discussing and pushing for profound and meaningful changes to bring about a better distribution of wealth and a more effective, dignified and just economic and social policy. **Today's politicians are just like anybody else.** They were chosen for various reasons to carry out a set responsibility, but they often lack either the ability or the honesty required to find solutions and alternatives to problems, and therefore look to improvise.

Cuts in public services, the systematic attack on democratic unions and the restructuring of the public and private sector workforce are some of the solutions that governments in many parts of the world have been imposing upon the working classes. Corporations and their allies have taken advantage of every opportunity to pursue tax cuts and to limit workers' and union rights.

Fortunately, we large unions and international federations have been studying, making proposals and fighting for a sea-change in this trend; putting the interests of the majority of the population ahead of those of the few. The latter defend themselves by exerting their influence and power over weak and conservative governments, as well as by mobilizing the media – which they also control – to undermine our arguments and thereby weaken the chances of any change to the prevailing system of exploitation.

The new model that has been put forward is that of Shared Prosperity, to rebuild economies, strengthen the middle classes and large population centers affected by poverty, create jobs, protect the environment and secure a better future for children, young people, women and the most marginalized communities. There are a range of strategies, policies and tools for achieving the Shared Prosperity model. Governments must listen to and heed these proposals, or they will be acting with serious disregard for the future of every nation.

The subject of Shared Prosperity was discussed in Toronto, Canada at *Workers Uniting*, a conference which took place over the 21st and 22nd May 2013, between the UNITE union from Great Britain and Ireland, United Steelworkers from the United States and Canada and the miners' union of Mexico.

Many governments have been losing the battle against unemployment and have failed to defend the interests of the majority of the population, leading workers and society at large to feel as though

they have been abandoned. Under the principle of Shared Prosperity it is proposed to reverse their strategy and for this we now need to invest in creating jobs and providing fair salaries; by strengthening – not weakening – labor laws, and by ensuring that governments provide workers' families with all the social security that they deserve.

The goal of Shared Prosperity was also the central focus of discussions and analysis during the international convention of the United States AFL-CIO (The American Federation of Labor – Congress of Industrial Organizations), which took place last week from 9th to 12th September in Los Angeles, California. **Thus, labor unions across the world have a global, constructive and purposeful agenda. Big corporations and above all governments should listen carefully, for everybody's sake.**

United for a Fairer World

With the above as its theme, the historic meeting of the Canadian Labour Congress was held over 18th and 19th of November in Ottawa, the capital of this surprising nation. Presided over by Ken Georgetti, the spearhead organisation of the Canadian workers' movement met with the leaders of the 34 largest and most significant trade unions, which together represent a body of 3.5 million union members. Once more, unconditional support for the struggle of the Mexican National Miners Union, Los Mineros, and its leader was reiterated, with an appeal to the government of Enrique Peña Nieto to bring an end to this irrational dispute once and for all, to grant absolute safety and protection for my return, thus allowing the historic miner's union organisation to return to normality.

The general frame of reference was inequality, anti-union labour reforms, and the persistent attacks against the workers' movement by the conservative governments of today's globalised world. Under this framework, it was highlighted that **many companies worldwide currently refuse to honour and respect their basic legal responsibilities towards their workers and operational staff**. The same thing goes on with governments, particularly if they are reactionary in nature like the previous PAN governments in Mexico, which protected and covered for the unholy alliance between official corruption and those groups most prone to cause disputes and opposed to significant change.

Right now, more than 70% of foreign investment in Mexican mining comes from Canada. The great majority fulfil their obligations, but there are other companies and some Mexican ones that do not respect the rule of law, because civil servants in federal, state and municipal government positions let them get away with it.

On a national level, obeying the law is something eminently simple, but it would seem many companies operating in Mexico find it very hard to do. These companies reveal their antisocial side whenever they are called upon to honour their commitment to the nation, whether it comes to the taxes and royalty payments owed to the country, their original owner, for extracting minerals and metals, or the fees for rent on the land that they themselves agree with the communities when they gain permission to exploit those natural resources, with little respect for the conservation of the environment. They refuse to honour these fair, legitimate and legal requests in principle, and only grudgingly comply when they are faced with no other alternative but to obey.

They gamble on the oversight or weakness of the state and communities alike, in the hope that at some point their challengers will forget and they will be able to evade the payments in question. This has lined the pockets of many mining companies, which nonetheless proclaim themselves socially responsible at every possible turn, flouting not only the truth, but the law. Thankfully the majority of companies in the mining, metal and steelwork sector don't shirk their responsibilities to the nation, but there are three or four very clearly identified companies that have been profiting from this situation for years, with flagrant arrogance as their benchmark.

At a meeting held in the Mexican capital on Friday 15th November, and **to the shame of many Mexicans** – congressmen, ruling politicians or just citizens –, Canadian legislator Bernard Trottier, member of the Canadian Parliament and director of the Canada-Mexico Friendship Group, declared that is the government's duty to create laws that favour the improved operation of mining companies within their national territory, and that in his country mining companies respect the environment, traditions and culture of the locales where they are based, as well as contributing significant resources, through taxes, to drive forward education, social security and public safety.

Every year – Trottier observed – mining companies provide Canada with 30 billion dollars (around 411 billion Mexican pesos) in tax revenues, resources which are used to promote education, communi-

ty development – also known as human development – and safety. He stated that Canadian companies are always expected to obey the laws of the countries where they operate, including environmental, employment and tax regulations. At the end of the day therefore, said Trottier, it will be up to the Mexican Congress to decide which laws they intend to put into practice.

The editorial piece in Saturday 16th November's edition of *La Jornada* newspaper highlights that "mining companies operating in Mexico, and the Canadian ones above all –Excellon Resources, First Majestic Silver, Fortuna Silver Mines, Continuum Resources, Timmis Gold, Starcore International Mines, Aurico Gold and Agnico-Eagle Mines, among others– have been the subject of many reasonable accusations for breaching the social, cultural and environmental rights of the areas where they are based, for systematically violating workers' rights and for enjoying disproportionate tax benefits and far more favourable conditions than in their countries of origin."

"Let us not forget", stated the *La Jornada* editorial, "that in the context of the negotiations around the recently passed tax reform, Canadian mining companies threatened to leave the country in the event of a green light being given to the creation of a special tax on exploitation profits… The position of the Canadian civil servant could be seen as a call to Mexican legislators and the state at large to exert its due sovereignty over this enormous fountain of wealth and become, therefore, beyond reproach."

The course, and the experiences of other countries, is laid out before us. Now all that's needed are the strength and political will to follow it.

The Geneva Meeting

The conference of the World Executive Committee of IndustriALL Global Union, the largest trade union organisation in the world with more than 50 million members in 140 countries, formally began on 4th December in Geneva, Switzerland, and continued throughout the Thursday 5th session in a positive atmosphere with great hopes for building a new system of relations of production, based on equality, justice and dignity. My presence as an active member of the World Executive Committee, which few had expected, created a charged atmosphere which raised everybody to their feet to applaud and welcome me at the beginning of the session, in a manner that was so emotive it is difficult to describe.

It was an unprecedented, historic event, with the meeting being held in the very headquarters of the International Labour Organisation (ILO) itself. For security reasons, we had maintained absolute discretion to keep my attendance a surprise until the right moment, following the absurd and irrational political persecution pursued against me by Mexican governments and their three accomplice magnates (Larrea, Ancira and Bailleres) right up to the present day.

In the official manner, the President of the Executive Committee Berthold Huber (Germany) and the Secretary General Jyrki Raina (Finland) welcomed me on behalf of all the delegates, emphasising that this was a moment in the organisation's history, bringing new hope, force and energy to us all in the enduring struggle for freedom and human dignity. They called the example of the Miners of Mexico, headed by me as their leader, an inspiration to the whole world, and described our resistance, bravery, integrity, heroism and intelligence as worthy of admiration.

I was immediately then given the floor to offer a message to the meeting's plenary session, during which striking solidarity was expressed by all, in condemning the repression, abuses of power, corruption and sickening political persecution used against Mexican miners, their leaders and families. My proposals were clear: firstly, we must prevent these acts of aggression from happening again, not only in Mexico, but across the entire world. Secondly, we have to consolidate a new model going forward, which we have called Shared Prosperity, whereby trade unions, companies and governments can coexist under a framework of respect, effectiveness, equity and general wellbeing for the working classes and society at large.

It is imperative to reduce or indeed eliminate inequality if we wish for long term productive relations and to live calmly, with social and industrial peace. The opening up of better opportunities to create decent jobs and fair wages, financial systems based on equality –avoiding the tax evasion of those who have the most–, education, care for our ecology and environment, and a state social policy geared towards regulating the economy with honesty and transparency, are fundamental to applying this new system or development model to the future of humanity.

The letter handed to me by the Swiss government is a work of art and legality, which enabled me to participate freely in the sessions arranged by IndustriALL Global Union, held in the impressive facilities of the ILO. **The immunity afforded to me by Switzerland honours its tradition as a free and sovereign nation that respects freedom and human rights. This is in addition to the policy of the government of Canada, which has welcomed me right from the start in recognition of my professional duty and fundamental rights**, offering me constant safety and protection, and indeed granting me residency with absolute respect for my status as a political and trade union leader.

The consideration and attitude of these two advanced governments of Canada and Switzerland sits in stark contrast to the false, mafioso and totally arbitrary attitude of the Mexican government, which in its eagerness to persecute me politically for being a progressive, nationalist leader, who challenges its nefarious interests, has shamed and discredited our country in the eyes of international authorities and organisations. **The triumph of democracy and justice in these developed nations will in**

turn be the undoing and frustration of Mexican governments, as long as they do not change their attitude and approach, and while they fail to pursue and punish the real criminals who loot the entire country on a daily basis.

For greater clarity and conviction, on Thursday 5th the World Executive Committee of IndustriALL adopted the following resolutions, among others:

1. To reiterate its unequivocal support for the National Miner's Union of Mexico and its President and Secretary General, Napoleón Gómez Urrutia. We thank the ILO and the Government of Switzerland for their assistance in making it possible for Napoleón to participate in our meeting in Geneva.
2. We demand that the Government of Mexico immediately cease its political persecution of Napoleón Gómez Urrutia, cancel the false charges against him that have already been repeatedly nullified by Mexican appellate courts, and guarantee the safe return of Napoleón and his family to Mexico.
3. The IndustriALL Executive Committee also unanimously resolved to nominate Napoleón Gómez Urrutia to receive the prestigious international Arthur Svensson award in 2014, named after a famous and distinguished Norwegian, which is awarded for outstanding efforts in the struggle to defend human rights, social justice, freedom and trade union autonomy in the world.

Finally, this meeting in Geneva, Switzerland, with the truth and dignity of the greatest world leaders, is a triumph for democracy, freedom and an historic warning of the failure of the world's reactionary, repressive and dictatorial governments.

A Plan for Productivity and Jobs is Urgently Needed

The growth of the Mexican economy, creation of dignified jobs, reduction in poverty and increase in external investment in the country call for a necessary reduction in violence, given that this is linked to rising organised crime and often to the recruitment of unemployed youth. All of this depends on the country's domestic capacity to generate wealth, and this in turn, depends on short, medium and long term growth in productivity.

It is a proven fact that **the country's productivity grows when we invest in education, research, training, science and technology**, but fundamentally it can only flourish if we recognise that this investment only yields positive results when we focus on human capital, on the men and women who are trained to innovate and produce the best quality, with greater efficiency and in concert with the current demands of the market, and its future demands of lower prices and higher quality.

The system of exploiting workers through capital must be consigned to history, and it is a system that Mexico neither needs, nor that suits investors. Investors look for productivity and competition, as well as the sort of great labour force that makes financial capital profitable, provided workers are treated with respect, justice and dignity.

The employer-worker relationship of partnership, communication and co-responsibility for success and productivity exists in small and medium sized enterprises, but is difficult and complicated in larger companies and multinational corporations. It is in those such companies where it becomes necessary for workers to join well-structured and responsible trade unions, led by professional leaders with viable and realistic social and economic policies. This is how a need for a new kind of global trade unionism is arising, which sits at the vanguard of achieving successful results, and is ready to contribute to the economic growth targeted through productivity and competition.

Anyone who persists with an outmoded mind-set does not believe that co-responsibility between trade unions and enterprises is possible, because it means trade union leaders become embroiled in the inner-workings of business management, and because both parties are condemned to the eternal fight over the annual revision of salaries and benefits. As long as the law of the jungle prevails in worker-employer relations and the rights of workers are not respected, the revision of collective bargaining agreements will remain a tool for fighting for social justice and balance between the interests of companies and workers. The fact is there should no longer be secrets in private management, unless the intention is to defraud the tax office and the shareholders. The old business maxim of keeping salaries as low as possible and exploiting workers is a vestige of the era of slavery that should already have been left long behind.

In its recent 30th March edition, London's *Financial Times*, an astute observer of the global economy, indicated that an effort is purportedly being made by certain public servants from Mexico's current government to increase productivity in productive sectors, but that they want to achieve this through bringing down wages, thus restricting demand and therefore growth, which can't succeed because this in turn means spending is not stimulated and the market shrinks. Additionally, according to the *Financial Times*, the supposed efforts to bring workers out of the informal labour market run contrary to the fiscal reform that taxes employers' contributions to their workers' benefits, which actually serves to incentivise the informal market, and also contradicts the labour reform that makes it easier to subcontract. Furthermore, the British paper adds that in a clearly contradictory strategy, the few truly democratic trade unions are being ignored, among which it highlights the miners' union, which was one of the first since the 1960s to sign productivity agreements that are genuinely aimed at collaborative working to improve efficiency, but meet with brutal repression in return.

As an aside to this assessment, **the analysis by the** *Financial Times* **contains an implicit call to stop living in the past.** It is important to recognise that real poverty reduction is only achieved through creating jobs and paying them well, which will improve the national economy along with increasing consumption. In order for spending to increase, wages have to be raised, the very basis of consumption and the economy itself. Mexican trade unionism cannot and must not distance itself from the dynamics, progress and challenges of global trade unionism. Many of the world's most successful companies have decided to incorporate their employees as partners, thus motivating them to innovate and increase productivity. **We need to be persuaded that work is not just a means of survival, but that it should be a way for humankind to pursue development and happiness.**

In addition to the historic workers' battlegrounds of the past, the workers of today are interested in matters as important as hygiene and industrial safety, health in the workplace, new skills development, housing and education rights for themselves and their children, the creation of stable, well-paid jobs, productivity and competition; matters that should concern us all – state, enterprises and workers, alike.

Women of Steel

To the cry of **'women united, will never be defeated'**, the First International Conference of Working Women began in Mexico City on May 2nd, against the backdrop of the General Assembly of the National Union of Miners and Metalworkers of Mexico. The strength and energy of this historic group was felt throughout the building and the whole organisation reverberated with their enthusiasm and real desire to become ever more engaged with the responsibilities and efforts of society.

They were calling, with every right, to be a part of political and academic life, of trade unionism, technology and general social activities, as well as for equal access to the rights and opportunities that the world has to offer. The meeting was coordinated by Carol Landry, international vice-president of the United Steelworkers union; Oralia Casso de Gómez; Lorraine Clewer, from the Solidarity Center of the AFL-CIO, and Julia Quiñonez, from the Border Committee of Workers (CFO, by its initials in Spanish).

To a greater or lesser degree women face discriminatory treatment in nearly every country, as if they were second class citizens. This situation calls for profound changes, and for greater justice and respect both within and outside of the home. **At the conference it was made clear that women are not victims, but contributors to social change and transformation who can open up new channels of participation and prosperity for the benefit of everyone in society.**

When women take an active role and are able to promote a range of activities from a place of peace without being threatened, challenged or questioned, professional and community work can advance and progress. Participation is not therefore a luxury, but a right and an obligation if women are to help build a new model in social and political relations where the rule of law prevails to ensure equality in all things, for men as well as for women.

In today's world there are clear examples of sea changes taking place through women being actively involved in productive processes, such as in China, India, Korea, Latin America and other places where **women have played a key part in modernization and raising living standards**. The profile of women has been raised in the United States, Canada, and Europe, predominantly in Scandinavian countries, through the opening up of new opportunities in public life and, more broadly, through fairer and more dignified economic growth.

These nations have seen the development of a more constant form of activism, using bold and intelligent tactics and taking advantage of key moments to bring about changes in people's mentality towards women and their image. The education and culture of men, but above all of women, have allowed a quicker and more dynamic march towards modernity, with fairness, justice and respect.

The message of the International Conference of Women was unmistakable. In this century, women need a new focus on transforming society and putting an end to the extremes of corruption, gender division and marginalisation. They made it very clear: now is the time to be heard and to express their ideas openly, because anything that hinders women holds back society as a whole.

Freedom and equality must be for everyone, man or woman. There remains much to do among the working classes to find new solutions and eliminate any form of discrimination. In efforts such as these, they said, there must be no limits, and this is the challenge. This is why women must be joined and we must be united in supporting our sisters. They asked us to remember that **women's rights are human rights, first and foremost.**

Lastly, the women of steel declared that they refuse to be stopped by the great tide of corruption that flows through Mexico and other parts of the world. It is evident that these courageous, intelligent and sensitive women are standing firm. They will not tire, and nor will the female miners, because their work for dignity, freedom and human rights is and always will be a permanent struggle.

Without doubt, their strength, effective and organised dedication, and the lessons and enrichment gained through new experiences will all help to bolster women's struggle for social equality, justice and dignity. This important conference will become the model for future meetings, which will surely open up new paths towards reducing inequality.

The Arthur Svensson Prize for Courage and Dignity

There are certain international prizes which enjoy credibility and importance on a global scale. The best known of these is the Nobel Prize, given each year to people who have most benefited humanity, or who have made a significant contribution to society. The recipients are selected every year by the Swedish Academy and the prize is presented in Oslo, the capital of Norway. There are various other awards made by other countries that are of real international significance.

Yesterday, on Wednesday 11th June 2014, I was most honoured to become the first Mexican and indeed the first ever Latin American to receive the 2014 Arthur Svensson International Prize for Trade Union Rights in Oslo, Norway. The award was granted to me by a group of organisations joined under Industri Energi, IE, a Norwegian trade union alliance that is a member of the IndustriALL Global Union, which represents 50 million trade unionists in over 100 countries.

The Arthur Svensson International Prize for Trade Union Rights is considered the Nobel Prize for trade unionism by the world's most important workers groups and federations, which select the deserving recipient. These include the aforementioned IndustriALL Global Union, the International Trade Union Confederation (ITUC), United Steelworkers of Canada and the United States (USW), as well as the miners union of Mexico and numerous other organisations from every continent, which jointly represent close to 200 million workers in over 100 countries.

Arthur Svensson (1930-2008) was one of Norway's most important social and political leaders, who as well as distinguishing himself as a genuine fighter for trade union rights, also promoted international peace, disarmament and a world free from nuclear weapons. Norway and other Scandinavian nations have the highest level of trade union membership in the world.

Svensson died in 2008 and in 2010 his Industri Energi group founded this award in his honour. The prize was created at a time of real trade union resurgence, following several decades when anti-trade union sentiment held sway within the context of neoliberal economics and globalisation, a phenomenon from which Mexico has sadly not recovered. This renaissance was a creative reaction against the imperial interests of the most economically powerful multinational conglomerates which had overseen repeated attacks and the decline of the trade unions.

In previous years, this prize has been awarded to some leading lights from the trade union movement, such as Wellington Chibebe, director of the Zimbabwe Congress of Trade Unions, and Shaher Saed, leader of the Palestine General Federation of Trade Unions. The decision to grant me the prize was made by 33 distinguished leaders and defenders of workers' rights. My nomination – as, according the prize committee, the "heroic **leader of Mexico's mining workers**" – was put forward in December 2013 by Jyrki Raina, leader of the IndustriALL Global Union, who then publicly announced that the award had been granted at this year's May Day march in Zócalo in the Mexican capital.

Industri Energi's decision to award me the 2014 Arthur Svensson Prize was based on the fact that "As a result of his vigorous condemnation of the industrial homicide at Pasta de Conchos, Napoleón has been persecuted by the corporate-governmental alliance. This persecution has, since 2006, forced this important leader to lead his Mexican trade union from exile in Vancouver, Canada. The Mexican authorities imposed this travel ban as part of a savage campaign against the miners. False judicial accusations made by the Mexican authorities have placed Napoleón on Interpol's red alert list since 2006. Although the miners have repeatedly succeeded in repudiating the false allegations, the authorities submit appeals and abuse the Interpol mechanism to prolong Napoleón's exile."

In March 2013 the red flag was cancelled by Interpol's secretary general and a renewed attempt by Mexico's Attorney General (PGR in Spanish) to re-establish it was rejected on 26th February 2014, **confirmation of the political persecution against me which casts shame on Mexico's image internationally**.

The 2014 Svensson Prize follows the prestigious Meany-Kirkland award, made to be in November 2011 by the American Federation of Labor, AFL-CIO, the most important trade union federation in the US. I feel deeply honoured by both awards, and they increase my sense of commitment to keep fighting for the rights of Mexican miners and metalworkers, and for the wider working class in Mexico and across the world, because I see them as recognition of the unbreakable struggle that we have built up and will continue to undertake.

I must point out how Mexico's media and press have pettily and almost entirely ignored the miners of Mexico and myself, with the sole, most honourable and brave exception of La Jornada and a handful of individual journalists. **It is obvious that certain powerful companies, rich in wealth but impoverished when it comes to social values and principles, have yet again silenced the media outlets they have at their beck and call.**

There are a few puppet journalists out there who have outdone themselves by trying to dismiss this prize, simply because of its recent creation on 2010. But soaring far above the non-existent moral quality of such people, the Svensson Prize is a grand expression of the dignity and solidarity of workers, which far surpass the narrow-minded reach of such commentators. Their only ambition is to blackmail Mexico's current administration to prevent them from justly resolving the mining conflict, unaware that defeat will be the fair and final outcome awaiting them and their anti-trade unionist masters. Victory is and will be ours. Svensson and the whole world know it.

The Politics of Pay: Unjust and Flawed

A proper policy on wages cannot be divorced from a government's employment policy and this, in turn, needs to be part of an overall strategy towards promoting economic growth. Such a strategy should benefit the majority, with new opportunities for all as opposed to a mere subset of society, as was the case in recent decades and has become even worse over the last few years.

By using a bit of common sense to look at what has happened to pay over the last 30 years, you don't need to be an expert or Nobel laureate in economics to realise that the outcome of adopting a model that was only designed to benefit the few has ultimately been growing inequality in our country, and the absurd and senseless exploitation of the workforce.

When it is said that wages in Mexico cannot be increased on a discretionary basis, or as the result of an urgent national programme to reduce poverty and stimulate consumption, we fall into a pattern which is not only unjust, but flawed. More so if such elitist, corporate proposals are backed by the authorities and, worse still, by trade union leaders who have no genuine concern for the wellbeing of the people they represent, even going as far as to sign an inexplicable Joint Statement of the Worker, Employer and Federal Government Sectors against pay rises, on 12th August 2014.

It is absurd to uphold a pay policy that has been failing for more than 30 years, a policy which is short-sighted and motivated by excessive greed for power and wealth, and which places the entire burden of responsibility and negative consequences onto the shoulders of workers, who generate the most wealth, but have the least. This selfish, limited and ignorant standpoint simply repeats what has not worked in the past, yet has increasingly led to capital accumulating in fewer and fewer hands. For the great majority, the counterpart to this has been dramatic growth in poverty and destitution.

This cannot stand, and no doubt the government is troubled by my proposal for establishing a new model that I have termed Shared Prosperity, which represents an entirely different and contrasting focus from the current system of growing exploitation and marginalisation. This is also why some members of the government want to link salary increases to the country's productivity, employment and economic growth. That is not the way to redistribute wealth under the prevailing model, but rather to concentrate it into the hands of ever fewer groups or families.

On the contrary, promoting consumption, demand and market growth and therefore investment, which in turn generates new kinds of work, is achieved through a policy of real jobs promotion – and there are many mechanisms for stimulating this – and with a clear and committed strategy for improving pay. The lowest incomes hold up the process and produce, as well as significant injustices, stagnation, recession and the subsequent delay of any programme of economic development.

There are many clear examples of this. Mexico currently has the lowest minimum wage in Latin America and probably the world, according to official figures released by the ECLA (Economic Commission for Latin America) and the ILO (International Labour Organisation). Lower even than Haiti and Honduras, where salaries are 56 per cent higher than in Mexico. Not to mention the comparison with China, where barely ten years ago wages were half those in Mexico, but today are two or three times higher.

The statistics don't end there: the average minimum wage in Canada is $10 per hour, and $7.50 for each hour worked in the United States is. In Mexico, the average daily minimum wage is 65.50 pesos, equivalent to $5 dollars per day. We're talking about a brutal difference in terms of full working days, whereby **a Canadian worker earns at least 100 dollars, an American $75, and a Mexican just $5**. How can a disparity as dramatic as 1,000 per cent be explained, when the standard of living in those countries is probably no greater than double or slightly more than the average in Mexico?

This is what we call exploitation, and a lack of care for or solidarity with the workers who generate the wealth, with Mexico and its people. In our country we have at least 7 million households on the minimum wage, which multiplied by five family members, means we're seeing 35 million people carrying out the lowest level of work such as cleaning houses and buildings, security jobs in residential areas or cleaning car windscreens, among others.

Political or economic analysis demonstrates that this does not stack up, whether rationally, or in human terms. Rather, it is clearly the product of an unjust and flawed model which has created greater inequality and extreme poverty, along with growing rates of malnutrition, disease, child mortality, premature death, frustration and resentment among the most affected members of society, which is the great majority.

How is it possible for a person faced with those conditions to have a fair and dignified pension, if the extra low minimum wage contributes 6.5 per cent of the retirement fund paid in by companies, the government and workers themselves? It will take around 30 years for employees to build up a larger pension than the one they currently have, once the minimum wage has increased. But as the great English economist John Maynard Keynes once said, in the long run, we are all dead.

A wage policy based on deprivation could have serious consequences for social stability, growth and peace. The low salaries paid in Mexico can be seen as a deliberate policy of exploitation and dispossession that has allowed a small group of more than 100 families to amass the greatest income, set against a population of more than 70 million poor people.

In Uruguay, Brazil and Argentina, pay rises led to an average increase of 20 per cent across all employment and 50 per cent in formal employment, precisely because of tax and financial schemes and stimulus for investment, **whereby the state grants financial breaks to reward each new job created and the resulting wage increase. Furthermore, increases in productivity in these countries have been linked more to the value of labour, rather than to technology, machinery, equipment, infrastructure or capital investment.**

Lastly, Mexico should observe, study and adopt measures from countries with successful growth policies, as opposed to obsolete and flawed models that only breed more poverty and marginalisation. The Scandinavian nations of Denmark, Norway, Sweden and Finland have experienced significant advances in the accumulation of social capital, with efficient and egalitarian strategies that recognise the contribution of people and their intrinsic value to the productive process, and this has had an effect on dignified and fair pension funds. Norway is a country with a population of 5 million people and one of the largest pension funds in the world, worth around $850 billion. It's about time corporate business owners, civil servants, politicians and trade union leaders looked to those countries and went on to speak and act with greater honesty and humility.

The Democracy that Mexico Needs

In theory, democracy is the form of state government wherein power is exerted by the people. Democracy is interpreted as a doctrine and a system for living within a society, and when it is genuine, it involves respect for human rights and the exercise of civil liberties in order to protect individual guarantees and to fight for equal opportunities.

This year will see local and national elections take place across Mexico, varying in scale and scope. Citizens will vote for the wholesale change of 500 federal representatives, as well as for different local councils and civil servants, along with nine new governors. In total, the National Electoral Institute reports that 2,159 public posts will be contested on 7th June 2015, the first Sunday of the month.

These are what are known as mid-term elections, because they take place halfway through the six-year period of federal government. It is well-known that these contests draw less public interest than presidential elections. That said, there is serious attention on participating in these political processes from a wide range of social sectors, as a result of the critical situation in which the country finds itself due to extra-electoral matters, namely the Tlatlaya and Ayotzinapa crises, combined with the drop in global oil prices, which has provoked sharp cuts in the budgetary spend for this year.

The working classes are aware of the developing build up to the elections. The importance of this national event on Mexico hasn't escaped our notice, at a time when the country is facing profound social and economic disarray. For workers, the political parties and the electorate have a good opportunity to suggest changes to the current political and economic strategy, a strategy which has concentrated wealth in fewer hands and made it apparent that popular demands are either suppressed or ignored, with government so far expressing no plans to alter the status quo. On the contrary, the upper echelons of power have stressed that this economic policy is here to stay, confirming their priorities and denial of the issue.

There is a very clear conception of democracy in the mining worker's profession, one which is expressed daily at the heart of the National Miners Union, Los Mineros. This has been a valuable training ground for this key, fundamental sector of national industry, where the issues of trade union representation and the management of economic demands are closely linked. It's an organisation where every single day, throughout the year, the way we practise democracy goes hand-in-hand with the need for economic progress. This is how Los Mineros, the National Miners Union, which I'm privileged to lead, has fought for and achieved the best and highest increases in overall income for its members, in the order of 12 to 14 per cent each year on average, well above the rate of inflation, but also significantly higher than those achieved by other trade unions through their annual salary review and collective bargaining processes. The key to this lies in our open and transparent internal political strategy, which we have employed to strengthen class unity, loyalty and solidarity.

This form of democracy, which builds on the basis of trade union organisation and achieves the highest levels of representation, has shown us that electoral democracy isn't enough if it isn't then reflected in improved wellbeing for those who work in productive processes and the generation of wealth. The same goes for society as a whole. **A system that remains purely electoral without drilling down to social and economic realities is an imperfect democracy, responsible for abuse and growing inequality.**

In such conditions, there will be little advance in terms of national democracy if efforts for the 2015 elections focus once again on the purely formal dimension of the electoral process. Many will question what has become of the democratic progress made in previous governmental terms given that people's living conditions and prospects aren't improving under this one; and that, on the contrary, the inequality and grinding poverty in which half of Mexicans live are becoming even more profound, something it seems won't receive sufficient attention at these elections.

True democracy must hark back to its modern origins, in the Enlightenment age of eighteenth century France. Montesquieu, Rousseau, and a little earlier Locke, along with many other thinkers of the time, clearly articulated the democratic challenge when faced with the authoritarianism of the monarchy and the lack of freedoms. In those distant days, **Montesquieu showed that love for the republic is the same as love for democracy, and that this in turn means love for equality, and "when virtue – the basic principle of democracy – disappears, the corruption of democracy begins and the republic is at risk of collapse". Thus, he said, the corruption of any government almost always begins with the corruption of its principles.**

As well as reading the French encyclopaedists, it would do the leading figures in politics, society and business much good, and those involved in communications too, to rekindle a love for service and for the nation. This would surely result in stronger efforts on everyone's part for elections that are not only clean, but which above all, go to the very heart of Mexico's social needs. A purely formal democracy, one upheld on a simply electoral level, doesn't mean much to people who are living with needs and wants that it is paramount, urgent and undeniable be addressed. It is a basic political imperative that we move towards a more realistic democracy, in economic and social terms.

Electoral contests that don't serve the economic and social betterment of the populous are merely despicable examples of demagoguery. Once a democratic system finally takes shape in Mexico that works towards the wellbeing, culture, dignity and happiness of the many, then we can be truly proud of our democracy – but not before then.

It's Time for New Politics

The AFL-CIO (American Federation of Labor), which represents 13.5 million worker members from leading trade unions, led by President Richard Trumka, held its Executive Committee conference from February 22nd to 25th, 2015. The events took place in Atlanta, Georgia at the Westin Peachtree Plaza Hotel, and I was invited to be an active participant, adding my contributions to those of other distinguished leaders, politicians, writers and intellectuals, among them Professor Robert Reich, author of 13 books and Secretary of Labor under the administration of President Bill Clinton.

The topics discussed are vitally important to today's world, and most of them have to do with growing inequality and injustices, as well as the objectionable practices of many multinational companies which try, together with conservative governments, to do away with democracy and trade union freedom of association.

There was a great debate related to the Trans-Pacific Partnership (TPP) treaty, which 11 nations – among them Mexico – are about to sign. So far, nobody knows the extent of this new free trade agreement, but by looking at the negative results of the one signed 20 years ago between Mexico, Canada and the United States, the great majority of participants were against it, because it would deepen inequality within and between signatory nations, because it is an instrument of geopolitical intervention, the hidden objective of which is to try to put the brakes on China's expansion, but most importantly because it will open up the floodgates to trade without limits, to the thoughtless exploitation of natural resources. It would have a direct impact on permanent employment and the unionization of workers, by making the labour market more flexible, meaning that companies will vie for cheap labour until it becomes a case of quasi-slavery dressed up as employment.

The trade union leaders in attendance expressed that when economic policy decisions are taken behind closed doors, this is done to shore up the preferences of the political and business elite, rather than for the benefit of the great majority of the population. Many trade policy strategies have long been made in this way, leaving workers, rural workers and farmers, along with small businesses and domestic producers, to pay a high price.

In today's world, trade agreements go far beyond imposing tariffs and quotas. More often, they are used to promote foreign investment, reduce barriers to business and widen support and distribution networks in favour of big retail chains and service providers. Trade agreements can have an impact on environmental safeguards, labour rights, incentives to socially necessary investments, food safety policies, as well as antitrust policies and many more besides.

This was why trade union leaders attending the Atlanta AFL-CIO conference expressed that when governments talk about trade policy, they need to ensure that the negotiation process is transparent, democratic and inclusive. Participating governments must avoid using their powers such as trade promotion authority (TPA), also known as fast track negotiating. It is more democratic to establish the direction and standards of the trade relationship openly, as opposed to imposing them in secret.

Delegates questioned the fact that fast track had never been used to promote increases in the minimum or average wage, or to grant full rights to women or even to open up free health and social security benefits, among other key issues for furthering gender equality of the general wellbeing of the majority of the population.

Thanks to economic crises, misguided commercial policies and a lack of opportunities to live and work with dignity, **the middle class in the United States has shrunk by half over the last ten years. If we look at the case of Mexico, equality has unquestionably suffered an even more significant decline**, as pre-existing problems have been compounded by the waste of public resources, a lack of safety, high levels of corruption and inefficiency, large debts and the weakness of public finances, as well as the crisis of image, credibility and confidence that is having a profound effect on the country. The Centre for Private

Sector Economic Studies (CEESP by its initials in Spanish) has already spelled it out: the complicated environment the country finds itself in is reflected in business leaders' uncertainty around investing. In its publication, entitled none other than "Crisis of Confidence", CEESP indicates that confidence is fundamental to economic performance, and calls for clearer legal regulation to lend certainty.

This is why it is the critical task and unavoidable duty of this Mexican government to prevent failure by respecting and enforcing the rule of law, and to do so with honesty and transparency. More than this though, and this requires a statesmanlike vision, the government needs to do everything in its power to improve people's general wellbeing and living standards. The key challenge is how to reduce inequality immediately, rather than increase it. The results of these efforts will determine the place the Mexican nation will take in history.

The Swedish Model in the face of Globalisation

A few days ago the International Executive Committee of the IndustriALL Global Union met at the Conference Centre in the city of Stockholm, Sweden, attended by members and representatives of more than 140 countries. The issues we discussed were extremely interesting, with actions and specific suggestions to stimulate growth, reduce inequality and lay the foundations for real development with less injustice and greater opportunities for the working class and the world population.

At the meeting the growing tendency for the concentration of wealth in the hands of increasingly few companies, regions or countries, a process that is currently going on in the international sphere, was made clear, as well as the conduct of large multinational companies that have eschewed ethics and acted with greed and unchecked ambition, and furthermore many governments that cover for them by granting them further privileges and concessions. The discussions centred around various countries and the global view, with declarations to prevent the violation of labour and human rights, as well as defending collective negotiation and rejecting the constant attacks on the environment, democracy and union freedom.

One of the conclusions was that it is necessary to establish a new labour and political strategy to force all companies and governments to act with greater social responsibility, to fight for greater justice and dignity for the great majority of the world population. We analysed the situation in Mexico with respect to violations of union rights and the system of collective contracts. Similarly, we analysed the situation of Myanmar as regards the change from military dictatorship to democracy; that of Ethiopia as an example of industrialisation in an African country; that of Georgia, the project to establish unions in a neoliberal climate, and that of China, the issue of how to to act in the face of an industrial giant that is constantly changing. Of course, we also looked at European economies and international bodies.

One of the highlights of the meeting of the Executive Committee was the participation of Sweden's prime minister, Stefan Löfven, who was previously leader of the Swedish Metalworkers Union (IF Metall), elected president of his Social Democrat political party and later as prime minister of this interesting and developed nation. His contribution was very well received as was the message he sent to his comrades of another era. In the end he decided to accept questions, and I spoke to give a comment and ask a searching question.

I began by congratulating him on his straightforwardness, which had impressed me, since in his response to every question he used our names, something that politicians do not often do, but he also had with him a very discreet security team. Secondly, I thanked him for his clarity and the ideas he put forward in a talk entitled Globalisation and Social Justice. He, in his answer, mentioned that the Scandinavian countries, and Sweden in particular, during the 70s and 80s decided to change their model of development to aim to include the majority of society in the formal economy, and provide more opportunities and greater well-being.

He emphasised that equality is the driving force for sustainable development. He pointed out that acting with justice and social responsibility, as well as treating workers with dignity and respect can generate higher income, in a win-win situation. He made it very clear that although this sort of model cannot be copied, what can be done is to make adaptations when there is political will to drive real development. There is no doubt that Sweden has become an example and an inspiration for many countries. Prime Minister Löfven offered to open the doors of his experience and show solidarity in sharing it. It would have a great impact if his advice were listened to and followed in Mexico.

At that moment I remembered, and mentioned to Prime Minister Löfven, what happened in Mexico 10 years ago at a dinner organised by the then president Vicente Fox with his wife Marta Sahagún at their official residence Los Pinos with four union leaders and our wives, as well as the Secretaries of Labour and Economy from his Cabinet. Fox asked us what suggestions we had for helping Mexico out of the crisis, stagnation and growing poverty. All those present fell silent, and I spoke to suggest that the government should study more closely the example of Scandinavian countries to understand how they had changed their economic strategies, left backwardness behind and became developed nations that are respected worldwide.

I mentioned that all of them, when they decided to change their economic model, through new policies, improved their productive efficiency, increased levels of consumption and investment through higher salaries, created systems of free education and health paid for by taxation, increased the level of unionisation (between 80 and 90 percent of all workers are affiliated with organisations) and drastically reduced levels of corruption.

In conclusion, by studying these success stories – I said to Fox – we could achieve a lot to adapt Mexico's feasible schemes. The response came quickly, but not from the mouth of the then president, but from his wife Marta Sahagún, who hurriedly said: "Well, that's a long way away". **My last comment was, "with all due respect, I'm not talking about geographical distances, but about examples to follow, not to copy".**

IndustriALL Global Union, a union organisation with over 15 million members, is playing an outstanding role in finding ways and methods that contribute to greater fairness, but at the same time fighting to contribute to the organisation of many young people and women and their active participation in a new global strategy that will surely bring good results in the near future. For me, personally, it is a clear example, even if reactionary businesspeople and corrupt politicians who have become a burden on society find it uncomfortable. And, to say the least, it is a great honour that since 2012 I have been elected as the only member representing Mexico on the Executive Committee of this incredibly vital organisation.

The Spirit of Social Democracy Spreads across the World

In recent months, a modern and advanced political current has appeared across the world, fighting in different countries to establish social democracy in government and yearning for a new model of economic development, one that generates greater justice and wellbeing for the population. Tired and frustrated with the huge inequality that we have seen, which today concentrates 99 percent of the world's wealth in 1 percent of the population, union leaders, intellectuals and progressive politicians are proposing ideas, specific strategies and programmes to balance the distribution of wealth and achieve greater equality and balance between members of society.

The aim of this is to defuse social and political conflicts, and to eliminate the exploitation and marginalisation that are seen across the world and which today are causing so many injustices and wars. These people and groups are committed to the ideals of democracy, freedom and greater social conscience, which they seek to achieve. This happened recently in the United Kingdom, where to the surprise of the ruling Conservative party and many members of that society, **Jeremy Corbyn was elected by majority as leader of the Labour Party, with a new vision of social democracy and the deep changes that need to take place in the economic structure of that nation.**

His proposals aim to reduce inequality, create a state that regulates and promotes greater investment and opportunities, as well as better supporting the working class and the majority of society. Corbyn's victory was seen as a refreshing change that renewed hope and inspired thousands of young people to join the ranks of the Labour Party, which they had abandoned in the recent past.

Similarly in Canada, whose Prime Minister is currently Stephen Harper of the Conservative Party, elections will take place very soon, on 1st October. Recent surveys put the New Democratic Party (NDP), led by Thomas Mulcair, ahead for the first time in history. The ideology of New Democrats is progressive, with a developed sense of social democracy and a clear commitment to the majority of the Canadian population and the country's working class.

Meanwhile in Sweden, Prime Minister Stefan Löfven, who was previously the leader of the IFMettal union, met a few days ago with the Austrian Chancellor Werner Faymann, and the German Vice-Chancellor Sigmar Gabriel, to finalise a plan that promotes changes to the new European Community Treaty, which aim to strengthen workers' rights. According to the Swedish government's website, the politicians, all of whom are members and leaders of social democracy in their respective countries, together with workers unions in each of those countries, analysed and negotiated a system to regulate and guarantee decent conditions in the European labour market.

European social democrats and unions are promoting a greater balance between freedom and rights, and they are convinced that free market economies, growth and the movement of capital and people, as well as goods and services, should not be more important than social rights under any circumstance. Today, most companies are in open competition to offer increasingly low wages and denigrating work conditions, as Stefan Löfven affirmed during the meetings. He concluded by highlighting to the Swedish TT news agency that there is a conflict between the competition and flexibility sought by companies, and labour and social rights, and that these rights should win out is the main objective of what they are calling the Social Protocol.

In other countries we are seeing a crisis of credibility and fractures in the economic system: in Brazil for example, ex-president Lula da Silva has suddenly come back on the scene announcing his return to politics. Lula was a national leader for metalworkers in that great South American nation, where he managed to reduce levels of poverty, create new and better work opportunities, turn his country into a powerhouse with a great future and improve the national image.

Pope Francis has condemned the inequality that prevails around the world, he has qualified it as immoral and has proposed a return to rationality through policies and strategies that are closer to the needs of the majority who suffer poverty and abandonment, and he of course suggests that the world should return to the ways of justice and dignified humanism. The Pope's influence is growing and he is always seeking to encourage the most needy and put pressure on those who have the most to share their wealth, respect people's integrity and recognise their right to a better life.

There are many other cases of leaders of academic, union, religious and political organisations in different countries which are proposing structural changes to the model of economic growth so as to transform it, through different strategies, creating systems of shared prosperity and greater equality.

In Mexico, the business class and insensitive conservative politicians seem to ignore the changes that are going on worldwide, because of course the last things that concern them are the needs of the population and the future of the country. They feel protected by their wealth and the unchecked accumulation of capital and material goods that they surround themselves with. However, it would be useful for them to recognise that reality is going to overtake them and their families, because thanks to their ignorance and lack of sensitivity, they do not realise that the ghost of social democracy, which acts against stagnation, inequality and poverty, will sooner or later catch up with them.

The New Strategy

In deciding to arrest the leader of the National Education Workers' Union, the current government has shown its determination to change the country, starting by establishing a policy of combating corruption and impunity. This is the clear message of one of the decisions that has most shaken up our country of late. However, this should not be indiscriminately directed at unions, which have faced the brunt of the basest instincts, but also at innumerable politicians, businesspeople, journalists and media, judges, magistrates and ministers, lawyers' offices, priests, chambers of commerce and others besides.

The President is taking such action because he made a promise to a nation tired of injustices, inequalities and a lack of rights, heading for failure, just as John F. Kennedy and Barack H. Obama have both made promises to the people of the United States at certain critical times. Moreover, Mexico has no other alternative and the worlds of politics, work, finance and culture are watching it. **Confidence is gained by raising the moral standards of a society and its government, and by correctly interpreting and applying justice, which must be transparent.**

Their ineptitude and corruption have meant that the PAN (National Action Party) governments led by Vicente Fox and Felipe Calderón have been condemned to oblivion and mediocrity. This new government has a unique historic opportunity, and by absolutely no means should it follow the path of the persecution and attacks on the working class and their honest, democratic leaders. They need stronger principles and ethical values than those of many of the people who are attacking the teachers' union. The message must be clear. It is not a question of political vengeance, but rather of a strategy to control runaway ambition and insulting opulence. As well as this, they must develop strategies, in other ways and in other spaces, to correct the irrational exploitation of the nation's natural resources through concessions and permits, blackmail, privileged information and trading in influence, which are only accessible to those close to the inner circles of power.

Justice must not be selective because then it is not justice. Therein is crux of the case of some corporate groups that have previously been named here, which pay little or no taxes, as exposed by the data published here in *La Jornada* by the distinguished columnist Carlos Fernández-Vega in January 2010 when he clearly identified a tax debt from 42 companies amounting to 223,707.9 million Pesos. This includes certain companies from the mining sector like Germán Larrea's Grupo México with a debt of 11,939.1 million, Alberto Bailleres' Grupo Peñoles with $6,124.14 million pending payment and Alonso Ancira Elizondo's Altos Hornos de México, which to date owes $6,666 million.

It would be very easy for the Treasury Ministry to demand the payment of these debts, which in many cases are confirmed frauds, going even as far as the non-payment of taxes upon the sale of businesses. Furthermore, some of these same consortiums have received hundreds of mining concessions and other sinecures, to the extent that more than 25 percent of the national territory has been given away in concessions to Mexican and foreign companies. That is to say, the hypocrisy of some businesspeople and certain media outlets has turned the strategy of media coverage and social attacks into a web of complicity in business and political influence, in both cases founded on the manipulation and confusion of the population. The truth is that very few of these assailants would pass the test of transparency and social scrutiny, because their hands are stained.

Some of these businesspeople are so cynical and heavy-handed that they talk about the politicians who are in power disdainfully and sarcastically, and they manipulate them to their own ends. They still take the liberty of announcing big investments that benefit them, so as to impress improvised and superficial politicians who when it comes down to it have no notion or feeling of how to identify and resolve social needs because they are only concerned with power and profits

and spare no love for Mexico. They are sinister characters who in one article I called 'bodies without souls'. In the political sphere we have seen the cases of barefaced corruption in recent PAN governments, led by Vicente Fox and Felipe Calderón, as well as some led by other parties.

As things currently stand, a single sector of society has been demonised: the working class. Many people forget that the unions have in fact, despite their flaws, been a force for balance, stability and social peace for many decades. They conveniently forget that workers have the right to act in accordance with the Constitution, the Federal Labour Law and International Labour Organization, and that union leaders are workers, just as the heads of companies are shareholders.

Mexico hopes that this high-profile case will be the start of a process of real change to eliminate or combat impunity and ensure that the state of law is respected, and not an isolated case. It is the political moment to establish a visionary strategy for the State, one that avoids unleashing persecution and the worst instincts of Mexicans whose frustration and impotence cause them to react in that way, faced with what is perceived as the lack of a better future for our country.

A New Economic Model, to Supersede NAFTA

Twenty years ago, on 1ˢᵗ January 1994, the North American Free Trade Agreement (NAFTA) between the United States, Canada and Mexico came into effect, which, according to one of its signatories, **the then president Carlos Salinas de Gortari, constituted "an historic opportunity for the nation to transform itself". Not only that, but if offered "an ideal way not to be left behind at the turn of the century"** and "to join a truly global community, an opportunity which, if taken, will surely mean the creation of thousands of jobs".

Thanks to NAFTA, the government assured us, Mexico would no longer be just an exporting power within the global economic context, but also a modern nation at long last, a player in the world's major economic block. Benefiting from the best of the agreements with the other signatory nations, it promised sufficient employment, a dynamic industry and efficient use of up to date technology, with an explosive growth in exports, better income levels, a highly competitive economy and an end to the migration of labour and capital. **In other words, our country would ascend to the ranks of the so-called first world.**

But the truth is that from that moment on, the Mexican economy has suffered deep changes which have disproved rather than realised the government's stated expectations. In the manufacturing industry, traditionally one of the most highly paid employment sectors in the country, with collective agreements that provided job stability and social benefits that improved the living standards of its workers, jobs were destroyed and declining employment and salary levels were recorded. But if we look at the whole period, this sector saw negative rates. Since 1987, the year that the privatisation of public companies gathered pace, a savage drop in employment was felt, in conjunction with the total opening of borders to imported goods in 1986, while still under Miguel de la Madrid's government.

Thus, 70,000 posts have been lost in the oil industry; 15,000 in electricity and 90,000 in mining. As to iron and steelwork, 23,000 fewer jobs have been recorded over this period, but 17,000 jobs had already been slashed in 1986, through the closure of the Monterrey Foundry alone.

Job security decreased over the 20-year period, which is directly linked to posts being cut in the most dynamic areas of the economy, and in turn to the wider decline in salaries and the resultant reduction in demand within the domestic market. Statistics representing the formal economy dropped from around 70 percent in 1980, to just 30 per cent in 2013, while the informal economy rose from 30 to 70 percent. This caused, among other phenomena, exponential growth in migratory trends towards the United States, where more than 33 million Mexicans lived by 2012, over 7 million of whom were undocumented, above all those from rural areas.

This dire picture was nowhere to be found in the optimistic vision put forward when NAFTA first came into effect. The Washington Consensus, a movement espoused by the developed world's major centres of political and economic decision-making in the 1970s and 80s –under the momentum of which NAFTA was settled and subsequently accepted by the Mexican government– showed not even the slightest concern for the fortunes of emerging nations, which included Mexico.

But beyond this, over this period we have also witnessed the weakening and general decline of trade unionism, especially of the democratic kind. This has had repercussions on the nature of employment throughout the economy, a global phenomenon experienced in every country where the so-called Washington Consensus vision was imposed. This vision was spearheaded by Ronald Reagan, President of the United States, and Margaret Thatcher, Prime Minister of Great Britain, in what was known as 'the conservative revolution'.

All these facts, however, generated a positive reaction among the most important unions in the United States, Canada and western European nations. Trade union strategy broadened from a purely national perspective to a global one, in the same way that the great capital cities had joined forces under a global economic agenda. This allowed the unions to gather renewed strength and bolstered pre-existing international workers federations, some of which went on to merge, giving rise in 2013 for example to the IndustriALL Global Union, which brings together more than 50 million members in 140 countries.

The National Miners Union, Los Mineros, of Mexico was always actively engaged in this process of worldwide trade union reinvigoration, to the extent that I, as its leader, have regularly been invited to sit on the global executive committees of those organisations.

It is fundamental that we continue to restructure the operation of trade unions and worker solidarity worldwide, through the permanent reframing of union strategies. **It is about building a new development model, which has been called Shared Prosperity, to ensure that the benefits of growing economic productivity, arising from the use of modern technologies, reach the people predominantly responsible for generating wealth: workers, and the population as a whole.**

The Fourth Industrial Revolution

The world of work has changed and, with that, the nature and role of the workforce have also been transformed. Many of these changes have had a devastating impact on the lives of workers and their level of social welfare. At present, the working class of Mexico is among the most dissatisfied, insecure, stressed and threatened in the whole of Latin America and other parts of the world.

There are two fundamental factors that have brought about this unfortunate situation. The first is the misguided employment policy and strategy that Mexico has implemented. In theory, Mexican labour law seems one of the most advanced, yet in practice non-compliance and constant violations under the indifferent or complicit watch of the authorities result in a very restrictive legal system which goes against workers' interests and tends towards the dictatorial in its abuses and corruption.

This is why it is necessary to change labour law, not so as to disguise or conceal reality but to create more security, justice, democracy and better conditions of production that would reduce inequality and benefit the economy in real terms. In all this, there must unquestionably be respect for workers' freedom of association and collective bargaining, including the right to strike, because without the commitment to abide by these universal rights, worker-employer bargaining is no more than a list of demands and a process of begging for what are the basic rights of the entire working class, which must absolutely be respected. Mexico therefore urgently needs an alternative vision to properly apply the law and put our labour policy right.

The second important factor which explains the transformations that have taken place in the world of work is the increased capacity for automation and artificial intelligence that today represents a threat to the security and availability of work in a way that has never before experienced. By this I mean that what has been defined as the fourth industrial revolution is having an equal impact on the manufacturing and service sectors of the economy worldwide.

The first industrial revolution occurred in the late eighteenth century, when industry made huge advances with the first use of machinery and equipment generating energy from water and steam. The second came in the early twentieth century when production lines quickly expanded thanks to the use of electricity. The third began from the 1970s onwards with the change from analogue mechanical production to electronics and digital technology, which revolutionised industry as a whole.

The term 'fourth industrial revolution' or 'industry 4.0' was first coined in Germany in 2011 in response to the rapid growth in the fusion of online with actual industrial production to create intelligent technology and precise timing to increase productivity and reduce costs. This was confirmed German Chancellor Angela Merkel during her message to the World Economic Forum in Davos in January 2015 when she referred to the 'industry 4.0 phenomenon'.

These changes represent a major challenge for all economic players and for the system as a whole. In the past, technology supported the creation of jobs, but now the new developments in computing and robotics are able to replace labour on a scale that becomes a real problem for the stability and peaceful progress so badly needed by society.

Jobs in the international manufacturing sector have been reduced by the attacks of automation, with the sale of robots growing 23 percent in 2014. Many of the displaced workers have been replaced by so-called 'trusted' employees, who have different labour rights to others, or those hired by outsourcing companies. In the coming years it is expected that sectors other than manufacturing will begin to use this new technology: the chemical, metal and energy industries, even using drones that replace humans, the automotive industry and others such as security, financial services and health.

The jobs that can be created by digitisation will be extremely sophisticated with machines controlling other machines, such that there will be few posts on offer and a highly qualified workforce, perhaps most prominently in the areas of the planning, configuration and maintenance new technologies.

Most of the jobs lost during the great recession of 2007-2009, which was even more intense than that of 1929, have not been recovered with human labour. Millions of workers have had to take low-paid, insecure and low-skilled jobs that many governments pretend is 'full employment'. Massachusetts Institute of Technology and the University of Oxford have predicted that between 35 percent and 47 percent of current jobs are at high risk of automation.

When governments analyse this situation they generally do so with large companies at their side, but never with the representation of trade union leaders. The challenge then for organized labour is clear, and we do not have much time or many alternatives. Unions and leaders must create methods, systems and policies through which technology can serve to create a better society and a healthier environment, rather than simply becoming a source of low-paid work.

Technology affects all sectors in one way or another, which is why we must urgently establish working groups to study, analyse and monitor these new changes ushered in by the world's fourth industrial revolution.

Anxiety and Fear

The surprising and unexpected result of the US election, with the victory of Donald Trump, shook the whole world and aggravated the uncertainty of many countries that have very close ties or are dependent on commercial, economic, political and migratory relations with that nation. And it's no wonder. The statements and threats made by Trump in his speeches and interviews during the political campaign were full of proposals that, if carried out, will create serious problems for Mexico and other governments in Latin America and the world.

Expelling 11 million Mexicans from the United States, with the consequent reduction of remittance income; building a wall along the border and cancelling or modifying the Free Trade Agreement, among other measures, would create serious problems for Mexico in assimilating these decisions, as well as further complicating the country's current unemployment and lack of opportunities. This is in addition to the political and social crisis we are facing as well as the growing inequality, marginalization and poverty that increasingly threaten Mexico's stability and peace. As such, despite efforts made by politicians and the major beneficiaries of these conditions, there is little room for optimism or for a superficial and indifferent approach this crisis which heralds a storm.

We could face an even greater dilemma which would result in handing over even more control of the country's natural resources, subjugation to the most shameless economic policy designed to favour American interests and the wholesale loss of sovereignty and autonomy of decisions of a government which ought, above all, to be free and democratic. The questions would be: are the authorities and groups which hold power preparing to assimilate or resist such eventualities? Or will they continue following the misguided strategy of manipulating the media and public opinion with the message that pessimism should not spread and that Mexico is prepared to collaborate with the new government of its northern neighbour, although in real life they simply try to justify or conceal what is happening? These are questions that must be analysed.

Around the rest of the world, in addition to the initial impact on the media, where there is plenty of speculation, and on the stock exchanges, **governments and right-wing groups feel empowered by Trump's election and are pushing for similar change through the upcoming elections in several countries**. In France, Marine Le Pen, presidential candidate for the far-right National Front Party, declared that Trump's victory is "the emergence of a new world", and that the same thing can happen there in the elections in spring 2017.

Meanwhile, Geert Wilders, leader of the Dutch Freedom Party, another far-right party, said that the Trump's election is a sign of hope for his aspirations, and proclaimed that a new order was born last week. He went on to say that a new revolution had been generated and that we are witnessing an uprising of peoples on both sides of the Atlantic. Wilders, who sports a blonde hairstyle very like Donald Trump's, attended several of Trump's campaign events in recent months. In Hungary, Prime Minister Viktor Orban, also a conservative, stated that it was a vindication of his struggle and his goals.

In Austria, Heinz Christian Strache, leader of the Freedom Party and a strong candidate to win the election on 4th December, said: "The left and the corrupt system, who see themselves as superior, have been punished and have been dealt blow after blow from voters who have forced them to vacate several positions of responsibility." Although France's Le Pen is the leader of the most prominent far-right group in Europe, all those of the radical right are now seeing their possibilities grow, as are many more around the world and in the politics of their countries.

We Mexicans must seriously, responsibly and deeply prepare ourselves to face the difficult times that will be result from Trump's election win the last week. And political, business and trade union organizations must begin serious discussions about the unpredictable consequences and make the necessary adjustments to their strategies if things do get worse, as we can expect.

Who Does Mexico belong to?

Little more than 30 years ago this question had a far clearer answer than we can give it today. In the early 80s there were over 100 thousand state-owned businesses that supposedly represented the interests of the nation and the people of Mexico. Back then there was still a nationalist project that sought to promote economic growth, create more jobs and contribute to improving the economic and social welfare of the population.

With the government of Miguel de la Madrid (1982-1988) this changed and the neoliberal model started to be applied in macroeconomic policies, deregulating the market, opening the economy to free trade and virtually unchecked competition and initiating a process of privatisation of parastatal organisations that has accelerated shamelessly during the subsequent administrations of Carlos Salinas de Gortari, Ernesto Zedillo, Vicente Fox, Felipe Calderon and the current government of Enrique Peña Nieto.

In other words, **in just over three decades the guiding role of the Mexican state disappeared and gave way to a nascent neoliberal scheme to transfer, sell, deliver or give away the ownership of resources and companies to private, domestic and foreign hands.** At that time, particularly since the government of Carlos Salinas, the role of the Mexican state was diluted with a very individual vision and an obsession with the concentration of power. This was not in a nationalist sense, but gave rise to a new generation of entrepreneur friends or associates of the president of the moment and an oligarchy which possessed wealth and influence never previously dreamed of, except in a few exceptional cases.

Complicities, frontmen, confidential information, concessions and influence trafficking arose in all their splendour for the benefit of a few.

Unprecedented fortunes have been accumulated under those practices, which run contrary to national interest and that of the majority, and the results today wound and offend the vast majority of Mexicans who are marginalised, poor and frustrated. No one currently knows with any certainty what happened, or how the public resources supposedly obtained from the privatization process were used. Those responsible still owe answers and the repayment of a social debt to the people of Mexico, who were, and remain, the owners of resources and the national territory.

Because this whole strategy was accompanied by an intense propaganda campaign which used the media to deceive and confuse everyone, we are still in a situation whereby complicity and joint partnerships between the new oligarchy and the media themselves work in an immoral system to betray the people of Mexico who elected the politicians involved. There are also sadly not many alternatives for the future of the country, apart from giving back to the nation, the true owner, what was stolen from it, but this seems idealistic, romantic and outside the the reality of the immoral world we live in.

So, who are Mexico's owners? The cynical and immoral politicians, ambitious and dehumanized entrepreneurs, political parties, transnational corporations, the domestic oligarchy, corporate unions, organized crime organizations, the Church, the people of Mexico? **Who really owns the country and its wealth?** This is a key question if we are to define the current state, direction and destiny of the Mexican nation.

On many occasions in Mexico we have seen the worst of human beings, and less frequently the best as well. We very rarely glimpse the generosity and solidarity of those who have the most, at the expense of the effort and sacrifice of those who have the least. Education, principles and values, morality and ethics, as well as the passion to serve and give oneself wholly for the sake of the majority, are almost nonexistent.

In economic activity and in politics the issue of inequality and concentration of wealth is fundamental and cannot be ignored. Equally the exploitation of labour and natural resources cannot be ignored, if the damaging effects for society are not correctly evaluated and quantified, both in the form and methods used by corporations to obtain higher profits even at the expense of the life and health of workers and employees; even at the terrible, often irreversible cost of breaking with ecology and the environment, or labour stability and peace.

Today the world and Mexico in particular urgently need a new, better and fairer economic model, as well as new laws and regulations that clearly define the role of the State and beneficiary companies as well as the rules and legal framework for their behaviour, while also determining and establishing their conduct and social responsibility, changing and correcting systems of production and wealth generation.

Although in reality all economic agents, businesses and government appear to act and relate directly to one another in society according to law, there are often relationships of complicity and corruption. In practice and in everyday life the law is not enforced and the rule of law is systematically violated, without seriously respecting the necessary political commitment and degree of social consciousness. As a result many entrepreneurs and authorities, who are generally the most dishonest in the country, act with great impunity.

By way of an initial conclusion on the original property of the nation, then, we can say we must either rebuild society and develop more egalitarian and social awareness, or the fate of our country will always be marked by inequality, marginalization, poverty and instability.

In remembrance of and with all my love to my dear sister Hilda Ruth.

Conclusion

Toward a Better Development Model for Mexico

The growth of the global economy over the last 30 years has created greater inequality and, in many nations, extreme poverty. The future of a country's prosperity cannot solely depend on a few people, individuals, groups or families, both for reasons of social justice and to ensure a fairer economic rationale. A model like the one we have now, which does not allow for any improvement in the population's standard of living, nor any increase in their purchasing power to stimulate demand and growth in the market, is a system that sooner or later is destined to fail.

It is important that we formulate proposals that generate new alternatives for the growth of the domestic and global economies, as well as for a fairer and more rational distribution of wealth. This is why it is essential that the criticisms, proposals and strategies contained in this book do not simply appeal to its readers, but can also be adopted and put into practice by governments responsible for making decisions and implementing healthy and balanced social and economic policy in Mexico and other nations.

The main purpose of writing this book was to contribute to improving the wellbeing of the majority, reducing inequality and opening up new and improved opportunities. The experience and knowledge gathered in these reflections could be of service to society, both the middle and working classes and the world in general, for continuing with the current system is not only increasing the chances of disaster, but also putting social stability and peace at greater risk.

This is why serious and profound analysis of what is happening is imperative, to look for answers that will help us to modify the status quo and transition to a more efficient, robust and lasting system of shared prosperity to benefit the great majority of the population.

There is no doubt that a series of economic and social policy measures need to change, along with fiscal, monetary, financial and commercial policy, to enable us to achieve an improved, fairer income distribution. It is of pressing importance that we adopt a new development model and a policy change that not only adapts to globalisation movements, but which also takes account of the social needs and rights of the community and the working classes. Various measures need to come together to accompany the process and foster growth in productivity and earnings, from more jobs and fairer and more decent salaries, to greater democracy and freedom, naturally alongside high quality education and skills training to improve the development of the workforce.

If this is achieved, we'll find ourselves in a virtuous circle where society's rules and behaviour have to improve, along with honesty and efficiency, in a world of greater prosperity and wellbeing for all. At the same time we need to rid ourselves of corruption, ignorance of laws and corporate arrogance, so we can find the way back to healthy growth, dignity for those who work hard everyday to provide for themselves and their families, and progress, and the path to decency that the enemies of the people have long since abandoned.

Donald Trump's victory in the US election on 8th November 2016 presents new and different problems to the critical situation that Mexico currently finds itself in. Without doubt, among many other conflicts yet to come, an ultraconservative government in our neighbouring country to the north increases the risk of mass deportation of Mexicans and Latinos, the attendant reduction in foreign currency income, as well as the cancellation or modification of trade treaties such as NAFTA, the North American Free Trade Agreement, and TPP, the Trans-Pacific Partnership. Mexico's government cannot remain indifferent to these changes that will affect us, and indeed the whole world alike. We must urgently face this new and unexpected situation with realism and patriotism, to be forward-thinking and strategic, to act with bravery and nationalist rigour, and to work together to defend autonomy, sovereignty and our nation's best interests.

The mining workers of Mexico have historically always been at the vanguard of social and political struggle, defending the rights not just of the working classes, but of the whole nation. We have the historical precedents of Cananea in 1906, Guanajuato in 1937, Nueva Rosita y Cloete in Coahuila in 1950, Lázaro Cárdenas in Michoacán in 2006, as well as Taxco in Guerrero; Cananea in Sonora and Sombrorete in Zacatecas in

2007, and in every region of the country right up to the present day. We miners have demonstrated pride, determination, honour and dignity in the constant struggle for the people's freedom and wellbeing, and we have demonstrated this to Mexico and the world, receiving recognition both nationally and internationally.

The writings published in this work were intended to denounce the abuse, corruption and impunity that sadly and despicably prevail in Mexico. The crux of its intent was not only to point out those responsible or the guilty parties, but also to propose changes and measures that alter the direction that the country and society are heading, to contribute to resolving the problems of the Mexican nation and other countries that find themselves in similar circumstances, by constantly striving for a better system to foster development, shared prosperity and responsibility.

In today's world, some business owners with an outmoded mentality, certain groups of conservative administrations and untold politicians believe that workers' organisations and trade unions are an impediment and obstacle to their interests, and that this is why it is expedient to replace those that currently exist with others controlled by companies, or to involve temporary rather than permanent members of staff. This is a senseless and short-sighted strategy that totally distorts the principles of production and the rules of fair and healthy coexistence, as well as equity among the forces of production, capital and work.

The economic growth model that has been pursued for the past 30 years has resulted in decisions that have viewed business owners and their associates as wealth creators, when wealth or real value is in fact generated by the workers themselves, the technicians, the designers and the operators in every manufacturing facility. This is why it is important to focus on new alternatives that already exist elsewhere in the world, and to use research to clearly demonstrate different ways of advancing development and progress, based on healthier and more stable economic foundations, which definitively generate greater equity and justice.

The proposals for the new model of shared prosperity will not simply be a theoretical statement or a definition, but rather a better vision for reducing inequality, improving wealth distribution and achieving a higher standard of wellbeing. There are clear examples of countries which have achieved productive efficacy, economic development, social justice, equality, the active and democratic participation of the population in decision making and a high level of organisation of their inhabitants, which shows that when we work in a consistent and disciplined way, with education that stimulates imagination and awareness, growth and a better future for all are possible.

Before we face a revolution that might endanger our peace and violently threaten the lives and wellbeing of millions, we must look instead to revolutionary ideas for nonviolent, lasting change. And in this search for a new way forward, we will find those clear and shining real-life examples in the world that we too can apply, which will enable us to finally achieve meaningful progress. So it is with hope and dignity, pride in our ourselves and our countrymen, we can look to the strengthening of our health and education, the solidarity in our unions with working and middle classes, our improved ethical behaviour as companies, our reformed political leaders who embrace and abide by the rule of law, and our nation, who chooses a path of prosperity not for the few, but for the many.

Postscript: Signs of Redemption

"Now this is not the end. It is not even the beginning of the end.
But it is, perhaps, the end of the beginning."
—Winston Churchill

As dawn broke on 28th August 2014, I knew it would be a pivotal day in my life.

Throughout a long series of battles I had continually proven that every accusation made against me was unlawful, and yet they had carried on pursuing a shameful campaign of persecution against me, a campaign first devised in the offices of Grupo México and the presidential residence known as Los Pinos, with the direct involvement of Vicente Fox and his wife Marta Sahagún, as well as Carlos María Abascal, Francisco Javier Salazar, Eduardo Medina Mora and many more. The day had come for the hearing, which would pass judgement on the last in a long chain of false allegations.

I knew I was innocent, and that gave me the strength to confront the sheer madness if it all, with many media sources of questionable ethics portraying me as guilty. Before that day, 28th August 2014, I had successfully managed to quash 11 charges of every type, all based on the same evidence, which in and of itself demonstrates the abuse that I was subjected to, and of course the violation of my constitutional rights by the Mexican government.

I picked up the phone and called Marco Del Toro, my lawyer who had been by my side throughout the persecution. My family was anxiously waiting to find out what would happen, along with my colleagues in the Miners Union. The judges sitting on the Fourth Collegiate Criminal Court of the First Circuit, Elvia Díaz de León D´Hers, José Luis Villa Jiménez and Héctor Lara González, would have to hear my case publicly, the latest in a long line that I had successfully fought, one by one.

This allegation referred, like all of them, to supposed unlawful management of the Miners Union Trust. They constructed an absurd charge of bank fraud, which is: "The undue use of the funds of a client of a banking institution." In order to articulate this, contradicting the very meaning of a trust, they declared that the clients were the workers and that I, along with other colleagues from the union, made use of their entrusted assets. **It was all a farce, but a farce that toyed with freedom, my freedom.**

Marco Del Toro had been making legal representations to each judge for several days in order to assert our position. Indeed, I remember warmly that on the last occasion before the judges pronounced on the case, he was accompanied by Dr. Néstor de Buen, who was the Miners Union lawyer for many years and an absolute stalwart of employment law in Mexico, not to mention an extraordinary human being. Despite his many years, Néstor went to see every one of the judges with Marco and advocated for me with the tenacity that only great men at his stage of life can display.

I smiled when they told me that he had seen two of the judges then decided to head on before the third when he remembered that his wife had arranged a march in Polanco to demonstrate against authority measures that they believed to be arbitrary. Of course he had to go. His love for his wife and his conviction to defend just causes allowed him to advocate for me and, thanks to his wife, to do it for other too. **That's what Néstor de Buen was like, an advocate in every sense of the word.**

My lawyer, Marco Del Toro, told me that the judges at this trial were brave, principled people who loved the law. This gave me certain reassurance. On the other hand I knew that Grupo México, its lawyers, civil servants from the office of the Attorney General of the Republic and the Federal Government, were all applying pressure on the judges, monumental pressure. Things were in the balance, and I wondered whether truth or power would prevail.

Mexico is a country rich in contrasts. There are great judges, but there are also quite a few easily biased ones, who the most corrupt business

234

owners and politicians are able to repress and control using their personal ambitions, rather than the correct and transparent application of justice.

Government authorities make boasts to other nations that we live in a country that respects the rule of law, but behind the scenes they contrive to construct unfounded accusations and political persecutions that are then echoed by the very media that they control, thereby supposedly justifying their poor conduct to society.

This last legal battle could bring an end to the war that had consumed so many years of my life. Events preceding this judgement made me think that my cynical rivals weren't going to give in and would do their very worst to keep up their disgraceful persecution.

In the weeks leading up to that day, various significant things and worrying revelations came to light.

In August 2014, the Assistant Attorney General Mariana Benitez went to the press to spread the word that the application to extradite me had supposedly been reissued. They had not counted on the fact that the very next day we would go public with the news that the Canadian government had awarded me nationality, precisely because – notwithstanding the efforts of the Mexican government – they were able to verify that the claims against me, which would be used to support an application for extradition, were entirely baseless. In fact, ever since previously granting me permanent residency, the Canadian government had expressly stated in writing that the Mexican accusations against me were not credible. **A real shame for our nation.**

I recall working with my colleagues and lawyers on the press release sent out at the time:

NATIONAL UNION OF MINE, METAL, STEEL AND RELATED WORKERS OF THE MEXICAN REPUBLIC

– BRIEFING –

Wednesday 13th August 2014

- CANADA GRANTS CITIZENSHIP TO NAPOLEÓN GÓMEZ URRUTIA

While articles continue to do the rounds in Mexico that show that some are still flogging a dying subject – in that the crime has been repeatedly proven nonexistent –; in Canada, Napoleón Gómez Urrutia, General Secretary of the Miners Union, has been granted <u>citizenship</u>. So, Canada is his second home, a country that opened its doors in the midst of a campaign of political persecution, a clear testament to the quality, maturity and solidarity of its people, trade union comrades and institutions.

On 30th June the complex process of granting Canadian citizenship was completed, although it was not remotely affected by the false charges – which were being defeated one by one in Mexico, precisely because of the inherent frailty of each of the baseless accusations.

Napoleón Gómez Urrutia now holds the legal status of a Canadian citizen. He naturally retains his Mexican nationality in accordance with article 37 of the Political Constitution of the United States of Mexico which specifically states that no Mexican by birth – as he is –, can be deprived of their nationality nor its associated rights when adopting a second.

Up to then he had held the migrant status of permanent residency, which was granted to him in writing, expressly stating that the Canadian government <u>did not consider</u> the charges made against him in Mexico to be <u>credible</u>. He was never a political refugee nor has he ever been a fugitive from anything or anyone, as has dishonestly been reported.

As the developed nation that it is – particularly in terms of its highly technically and ethically sound justice system – Canada has not paid any heed to allegations that were evidently false and identical to others which had already given rise to firm assertions of innocence.

In line with the international position, the governments of Switzerland and Norway also extended offers of safe passage allowing Napoleón Gómez Urrutia to enter their countries, with the guarantee that he would not be arrested even in the event that Mexico sought his extradition, which speaks for it-self.

Napoleón Gómez Urrutia enjoys all the rights of a Canadian national. He was in fact sent a letter welcoming him as a citizen signed by Prime Minister Stephen Harper, following a moving event and the presentation of his certificate.

It seems inexplicable to persist in spreading allegations that clearly form part of a campaign of political persecution, whereby he was charged on the basis of the same facts eleven times, and in ten of these cases received a firm ruling of not guilty. The last of these judgements is about to heard, and it is reasonable to expect that it will also clearly establish his innocence.

In Mexico, Napoleón Gómez Urrutia retains all his rights as a Mexican. He will continue to conduct his leadership in his characteristic style: vertical, upstanding and protective of workers' right, which ironically was the initial cause of the political persecution that he has faced. Naturally, aware of the need to secure the tasks he undertook to improve the situation of the workers of the Miners Union, he is preparing his return so that he can consolidate the projects that have been going on productively in his absence, like the Mexican that he so proudly is – in defiance of all those who thought he would throw in the towel given all the attacks that have been made against him and which have failed in the courts.

The international community has, with evidence, rejected this persecutory campaign motivated by political and economic interests. Meanwhile in Mexico, biased information continues to circulate which could incur legal liability for those who falsely propagate it, whether for personal or political reasons.

This recently granted Canadian citizenship strengthens the links between the miners of both nations and makes it clear that truth should always prevail over darker interests, and solidarity over irrational persecution.

But that wasn't all: Felipe Calderón's government managed to obtain an Interpol red notice, by manipulating false and unlawful information. This led my legal team to undertake two different courses of action:

In Mexico, Marco Del Toro, working alongside David Martin, a distinguished Canadian lawyer, drew up a legal submission to protect me against the Interpol red notice, which was sent at the request of the Attorney General's Department for International Affairs and Interpol.

In Lyon, France, home to the international policing agency's headquarters, an application to cancel the red notice was submitted to the Commission for the Control of Interpol's Files. This was based on the premise that Interpol Mexico had provided false data to initiate the red notice, as well as its clear political grounds that rendered it illegal, and I confirmed the shameless persecution in my letter.

Both efforts succeeded. We managed to assert that the red notice was based on lies, politically motivated and should therefore be cancelled.

The order to cancel the red notice was issued in both Mexico and France. I can remember the feeling when I was told that the Interpol Commission had determined that the application for the red notice included false information and could be seen to be politically motivated. After analysing all the documents sent by Mexico and in particular those submitted by my lawyers, they were able to reach this conclusion. I've been told that this does not often happen. Interpol is a highly esteemed global organisation, which is why its resolution left it patently clear that Mexico was harassing me without any grounds, based on factors that had nothing to do with the law.

It's sad to see that Mexico, as a country, can keep on fabricating this sort of witch-hunt. It is such a shame that it has to be foreign authorities – such as the Canadians, Swiss or Norwegians, as well as Interpol International – who have been the ones to expose this sham concocted from behind closed doors by the Mexican authorities and the business owners who loom larger than anyone would imagine in their decision making.

Let us not forget Canada's remarkable resolution in which it expressly stated that it had granted me citizenship because the allegations made against me by Mexico were not credible, and because I met all the requirements of a distinguished member of their nation.

As soon as he heard the news, Jack Layton, the honourable leader of the New Democratic Party (NDP), called me personally and said "Congratulations my friend, welcoming a partner of such education and integrity who will really enrich our country, is Mexico's loss and Canada's gain. We'll have to celebrate with Olivia, Oralia and our good friends like Leo Gerard and Ken Neumann. All the best, and welcome."

With everything that had happened so far, it seemed as though the final charge, which had yet to be neutralised, was going to endure unimaginable pressure in its attempts to keep me in its sights. It was a very nervous morning for my colleagues, and me with constant calls to Marco Del Toro. Still there was nothing, no word from the judges on a decision, and every passing minute felt like a year.

I knew that Marco Del Toro and some lawyers from his team were at court, accompanied by various members of the National Executive Committee of the Miners Union. We were all feeling hopeful, but also worried. They called me and told me that representatives from the Attorney General's office were there too, along with Grupo México's legal team. The pressure facing the judges was absolutely immense. Just when it seemed as though they were about to hear my case I got a call telling me that the judges had gone for lunch and the court was in recess, meaning the uncertainty was prolonged for yet more hours. The afternoon drew on in Mexico, with me continuing to hold on in Canada, waiting and waiting, although in my heart of hearts I felt a certain calmness; despite all the corrupt pressures and interests, I trusted that the truth would prevail, as finally came to pass.

At around five in the afternoon, Mexican time, Marco Del Toro finally called, his voice noticeably moved. "We won, it's over. A unanimous decision. Innocent."

I felt a very special kind of satisfaction that you can only really experience if you have been in a similar situation. Years of uncertainty, legal battles, pressure, defamation and an unprecedented and shameful campaign of political persecution were finally behind me. It was a historic decision for my family, for the Miners and indeed for all Mexicans, which laid bare the paucity and shamefulness of the PAN party governments of Vicente Fox and Felipe Calderón, along with the pitiful businessmen and civil servants manipulated and led by the morally bankrupt Grupo México company and the cronies and accomplices of Germán Feliciano Larrea Mota Velasco, its president.

Marco explained to me that the three judges had debated the matter and gave their legal opinion on it one by one, and that this took place in the public hearing attended by lawyers from the Attorney General's office and the companies, but also colleagues from the Miners Union and members of our defence team. They told me that when the verdict was passed, when the judges voted, there was an outpouring of emotion and my lawyers and colleagues embraced one another. They had to leave the room so as not to interrupt the judges with the following hearing on other matters.

I asked Marco del Toro if we could speak again in a few minutes, to give me time to tell my wife and children. I picked up the phone and called Oralia right away, who was calmly waiting to hear the court's decision.

On this important day, my wife had been invited by a group of friends to meet up in an incredible place to the north of Vancouver, but she wasn't sure whether to go. She knew that the decision of the Fourth Collegiate Court of the National Supreme Court of Justice was due to be announced that day, which would finally determine my legal status, something which had so unjustly embroiled my family, through no fault of their own.

Through ambition, greed, corruption and spite, Larrea, Fox, Marta Sahagún and the whole mob of Grupo México's cronies and hangers-on had all become sheer criminals who wouldn't even stop at attacking our family. It's disgraceful to think that these individuals were in charge of the country and that many people showed them real deference, unaware of the kind of thugs and criminals that they really were.

I insisted and finally convinced Oralia, my great companion in life and in the struggle for a fairer, more decent Mexico, to go and take her mind off things with her friends. A change of scenery, even if just for a day, to stop thinking about the monsters who were behind this attack on mining families and all of Mexico, the country that they had been using and would continue to use solely for their own personal gain as individuals or as a group.

So, as soon as I got the call from Marco with the good news, I rang Oralia first and told her "I want you to stay calm as I'm about to give you some news… WE WON!" The court's decision was unanimous, firm and definitive and had completely exonerated me from this whole dreadful campaign of attacks, lies and false allegations, the product of the sick and deranged minds of a few sinister characters.

My dear Oralia, who was at the end of her get-together with friends, remained quiet for a minute, and I imagined everything that could be going through her head at that very moment, from the enforced exile from Mexico, to the constant, dirty attacks in the media, paid for by the same pathetic and miserable group, and that now, suddenly, after a tremendous, fierce fight for justice, we had overcome. She broke down and was overcome with tears of joy at the table surrounded by her friends, who had no idea at all what was happening. Oralia then replied, "Thank you for this wonderful news, I feel at peace and as though I can finally breathe out - for you, for my children and for the whole family; and of course for all the brave and loyal miners and international leaders who always believed in you and who supported you so unconditionally."

"I always believed in you, I knew that you were going to win sooner or later, because the truth would out, and I feel so, so proud of your attitude throughout all this. You are the best, you beat them because you a strong, proud, very brave and fearless man, and you faced up to a corrupt system that could never destroy your integrity, bravery, wisdom and intellect. Congratulations, my love…!"

We ended the call, and she later told me that her friends hadn't understood a word, but they immediately hugged her and asked her if something bad had happened and she replied that no, she was crying from happiness because she had just received the most extraordinary news that she had been waiting for, for a long time. I went straight on to speak to each of my three children to tell them about the court's ruling that Marco and my colleagues had shared with me. They were all delighted with the final decision, and they all felt overcome with a deep sense of safety, coupled with caution, since each of them had lived through and suffered the consequences of this baseless attack as well as a dirty, twisted campaign by the media, which unfortunately manipulates public opinion in Mexico.

These actions and decisions, which were the result of ignorance, corruption and arrogance, must never happen again, not here in Mexico nor anywhere else in the world. The country, its laws and the moral obligation of respect, justice and dignity for Mexicans, need to be a permanent, non-negotiable undertaking, less subject to a small group of corrupt people, full of complexes, fears, suspicion and self-doubt, in order to steer the country.

Either Mexico changes, or circumstances will overtake us. If that happens, the levels of violence, poverty, inequality and injustice experienced on a daily basis in this country will be indescribable.

No more Pasta de Conchos disasters, no more aggression, no more violations of the integrity and honour of Mexicans and the true leaders who are waiting for the chance to serve their country, with sincerity and honesty. This corruption and this obsessive and cowardly violence, has to and surely will come to an end. Mexico and the Mexican people cannot and must not be subject to the whims of a group of exploitative individuals who have abused this great country's kindness. We have already put down a marker, and we won't stop until the end, for this is the destiny of this great nation.

As our euphoria settled down into serenity, we decided to send out a press release, which I will leave here for posterity:

NAPOLEÓN GÓMEZ URRUTIA IS DEFINITIVELY DE-CLARED INNOCENT

NAPOLEÓN WON, LARREA AND GRUPO MEXICO LOST

One of the most arduous and bloody battles in the legal history of Mexico has come to an end. Yesterday, August 28th 2014, the judges of the Fourth Collegiate Criminal Court of the First Circuit, Elvia Díaz de León D´Hers, José Luis Villa Jiménez and Héctor Lara González, unanimously resolved to rule that the last of eleven arrest warrants issued to the General Secretary of the Miners Union, Napoleón Gómez Urrutia, was unconstitutional.

In a public hearing with the courtroom packed with spectators, the judges analysed case 121/2014, which was initiated by the appeal lodged by the mining union leader's legal defence team.

After extensive discussion, they issued a sentence through which the Federal Judiciary granted protection to Gómez Urrutia, cancelling the arrest warrant for a serious offense under the Law of Credit Institutions related to the dissolution and management of the Mineworkers Trust and the resources entrusted to it in the sum of $55 million.

The government of Mexico must now immediately inform its counterparts in Canada that the wrongful request for extradition based on false evidence, which has been pending since 2008 and was recently reinforced by the Assistant Attorney General for International Affairs, Mariana Benitez Tiburcio, is definitively without effect. Similarly, the Attorney General's Office must notify the Interpol headquarters in Lyon, France that it should proceed to remove the red notice which was issued despite its own assessment last February that it formed part of a campaign of political persecution orchestrated in Mexico against the General Secretary of the Miners Union.

The eleven arrest warrants that had been hanging over the mining union leader have now been cancelled. This final ruling means that Napoleón Gómez Urrutia is now able to return to Mexico in absolute freedom, which Mexican miners are celebrating.

Marco Del Toro, the lawyer who defended all of the criminal cases and extradition requests, said: "Over many years of defence I have observed and can now confirm that in Mexico there are examples of judges who resist the most tremendous pressures, upholding the law and putting the honourable function they perform before interests unrelated to the values that inspire their daily duties on behalf of the Nation; paying great testimony to their names and their careers. I am delighted that the law, to which I have dedicated a large part of part of my life, has been the instrument capable of putting an end to a persecution in which political and economic interests conspired in a groundless attempt to imprison Napoleón Gómez Urrutia. This has certainly reinforced my vocation as a defence lawyer."

It seems inconceivable and almost paranoid to believe that a company like Grupo México, owned by Germán Feliciano Larrea Mota Velasco, fabricated baseless criminal charges through the use of three fake mining workers, charges which were then wrongly supported as part of a clear strategy of political persecution by the governments of Fox and Calderón – and even by some junior officials of the current administration, presumably motivated by specific and obscure interests that are not aligned with the policies of the Presidency of the Republic. It is also inconceivable that this businessman continues to cause human, economic and environmental disasters, thinking that he is above the law and can continue in a state of impunity as he has up until now.

With the criminal case wrongly contrived by Grupo México reaching its conclusion, our aim now will be to meet with representatives of the highest levels of government so that the Miners Union and its General Secretary can contribute, through a framework of mutual respect, to the development of our industry and the defence of workers' rights, as well as the wellbeing of them and their families.

We thank the members of our national mining union for their support, global trade union organisations, and political, human rights and non-governmental leaders who have demonstrated their solidarity and worked with us *to fight this unprecedented political persecution, which should now be relegated to the past.*

In the coming days, the General Secretary of the Miners Union, Napoleón Gómez Urrutia, will hold a press conference alongside people of various nationalities in *which he will discuss his position in light of the conclusion of this dark episode in the legal, social and political life of the country.*

I knew that the judges were worried that day, and that they had been under pressure from calls from high up in the Attorney General's office. I also knew that Grupo México had made attempts to influence their decision. But they resisted in spite of all this, and so they can face their families and the Mexican people with pride. **They are true judges, not like others who take on the office with ulterior motives which corrupt their duties.**

From that moment on, we have called for the state and some of those who slandered us to take responsibility. We have also heard

about attempts to reignite the allegations against me, all without any grounds.

The next step is to return to Mexico, once we can be certain that they do not have some dark, twisted ace up their sleeve. After all, we had been forced to defend ourselves against the same charges eleven times over.

I will not stop making demands and pointing the finger when the circumstances merit it, as was the case with the terrible spill caused by Grupo México in the river Sonora, the company's second act of 'industrial homicide', when 400 million litres of highly carcinogenic chemical substances were spilled, making it the worst tragedy in the history of Mexican mining.

I will continue to make life difficult for those who attack the integrity of my mining colleagues. Rivers of ink were spilled in the attempts to have me charged, but I knew that Mexico is a great country full of valiant people who live alongside a few who have learned how to grab power through manipulation, influence peddling, corruption and exploiting confidential information to gain access to permits and concessions, which they use for their own ends and to the detriment of others.

I learned that there are judges and magistrates with conviction, but there are also some that are easily influenced.

I also learned that there are lawyers who only think about their pockets; who even go so far as to steal from their clients. But that there also others like Néstor (RIP) and Carlos de Buen, David Martin, Juan Carlos Hernández and his late father and, of course, Marco Del Toro. These lawyers faced up to the many-headed beast; they did it without anything close to the resources their opponents had, and they came out with their heads held high.

I learned that by fighting using legal and political means, it is possible to topple someone who falsely accuses you, even if they are more powerful than you. Of course, you might have to wait for years that you'll never get back and endure anxiety that no one should ever have to suffer. At the end of the day, this is Mexico... this is the Mexico that we have to change, to educate with principles and values to bring about an intellectual, cultural and moral revolution, so we can return to the times of calm, peace and opportunity that were taken away from us by a handful of thieves, who I am sure will, sooner or later, face justice.

the damaging effects for society are not correctly evaluated and quantified, both in the form and methods used by corporations to obtain higher profits even at the expense of the life and health of workers and employees; even at the terrible, often irreversible cost of breaking with ecology and the environment, or labour stability and peace.

Today the world and Mexico in particular urgently need a new, better and fairer economic model, as well as new laws and regulations that clearly define the role of the State and beneficiary companies as well as the rules and legal framework for their behaviour, while also determining and establishing their conduct and social responsibility, changing and correcting systems of production and wealth generation.

Although in reality all economic agents, businesses and government appear to act and relate directly to one another in society according to law, there are often relationships of complicity and corruption. In practice and in everyday life the law is not enforced and the rule of law is systematically violated, without seriously respecting the necessary political commitment and degree of social consciousness. As a result many entrepreneurs and authorities, who are generally the most dishonest in the country, act with great impunity.

By way of an initial conclusion on the original property of the nation, then, we can say we must either rebuild society and develop more egalitarian and social awareness, or the fate of our country will always be marked by inequality, marginalization, poverty and instability.

In remembrance of and with all my love to my dear sister Hilda Ruth.

Conclusion:
Toward a Better Development
Model for Mexico

About the Author

Napoleón Gómez has been General Secretary of the National Union of Mining, Metallurgical, Steel and Allied Workers of Mexico, known as Los Mineros, since his unanimous election in 2002. He was re-elected for a new term in 2008 and named President in 2012. An economist, he graduated with honours from the Universidad Autónoma Nacional of Mexico and from Oxford University. In 2011, Gómez Urrutia received the prestigious Meany-Kirkland Human Rights Award from the AFL-CIO, and in 2014 he was honoured with the highest international distinction given in labour rights, the Arthur Svensson Prize in Norway. In 2014 he received the distinguished IPPY gold medal, presented by the New York Association of Independent Publishers, for his New York Times bestselling book Collapse of Dignity: and the fight against greed and corruption in Mexico. He was also awarded the renowned 'Emilio Krieger' Medal in 2014 by the National Association of Democratic Lawyers (ANAD, its initials in Spanish). That same year he received the prized "Sentiments of the Nation" Medal, granted by the Popular Assembly of the Peoples of Guerrero (APPG, its initials in Spanish). He serves as a member of the Executive Committee of IndustriALL Global Union, the world's largest and most powerful global trade union. He works very closely with the leaders of trade union organisations from various countries, including the United Steelworkers.

He previously spent 12 years as General Director of the Casa de Moneda de México (National Mint of Mexico)and was elected International President of the Mint Directors Conference, he is only Mexican to have ever held to this highly distinguished position.